Practicing the
Monastic Disciplines

Practicing the
Monastic Disciplines

Finding Deep Spirituality in a Shallow World

SAM HAMSTRA JR.
and SAMUEL COCAR

WIPF & STOCK · Eugene, Oregon

PRACTICING THE MONASTIC DISCIPLINES
Finding Deep Spirituality in a Shallow World

Wipf & Stock
An Imprint of Wipf and Stock Publishers
199 W. 8th Ave., Suite 3
Eugene, OR 97401

www.wipfandstock.com

PAPERBACK ISBN: 978-1-7252-9360-1
HARDCOVER ISBN: 978-1-7252-9359-5
EBOOK ISBN: 978-1-7252-9361-8

07/01/21

Contents

Preface

SAM HAMSTRA JR.

If as a devoted Christ-follower you are serious about personal spiritual transformation, you will want to know more about the desert tradition, in general, and about Evagrius the Solitary, in particular. While relatively unknown in American Protestant circles, Evagrius of Pontus (345–399) is one the more important names in the history of Christian spirituality and his writings are among the more interesting works of Christian antiquity.[1]

For the past few years, I have done a deep dive into Evagrius and the broader desert tradition. Thankfully, I have been aided in my journey by some outstanding Christians who, with scholarly precision and spiritual passion, introduced me to a mostly forgotten stream of Christian devotion. There are reasons for this amnesia, most notably the accusation of heresy. True or false, the accusation alone will stick with you for centuries. Sixth-century councils condemned the teachings of Origen and his pupil, Evagrius (though not by name). Then there is the supposed disconnect between a Christian living in a desert and a Christian living in a twenty-first-century American city. How can an ancient desert monk help me face and defeat the temptations I face each day?

As I reflected on this question of modern relevance, several thoughts came to my mind. I share them hoping they are not generated by the thought of vainglory. First, even though I am a Christ-follower and a temple of the Holy Spirit, I remain a sinner. In fact, my default is sin. Daily I engage in

---

1. See John Eudes Bamberger on the recovery of the Evagrius writings in his introduction to Evagrius, *Praktikos*, xxiii–xxxv.

both inner and outer spiritual warfare. Internally, I wrestle with "the lust of the eyes, the lust of the flesh, and the pride of life" (1 John 2:16). Externally, I wrestle with both personal and systemic evil. Individuals attack me and those I love. Systems flaunt themselves before my eyes even as I drive my car down the highway, where billboards invite me to detour from my destination for a supposedly meaningless rendezvous with strip clubs, gambling, or other forms of mindless consumption. Plus, Satan himself roams my streets, even my church, seeking those whom he can devour.

Furthermore, while the Lord has been and will be my refuge and strength as I battle with temptation, I still don't trust myself. This wariness of the self, of the ego, should apply to all apprentices of Jesus. In that well-worn passage from Jeremiah, we learn that "The heart is deceitful above all things, and desperately sick; who can understand it?" (Jer 17:9, ESV). We indeed ought to fear entering the spiritual battlefield empty handed, without the spiritual arsenal by which to defeat temptation. So, I am looking for ways to rest in the gracious provision of the Lord while cooperating with the Holy Spirit so that I can grow in Christlikeness—that is, experience continuous spiritual transformation.

Those thoughts intersected with my study of the ancient desert monk named Evagrius. As Jean Leclercq predicted, "Simple men of God recognize in his writings a description of their own problems and difficulties and also discover solutions to them."[2] Consequently, lay men and women, even Evangelicals like me, may draw as much profit from Evagrius as monks and nuns, historians and scholars. Most significantly for me, Evagrius hammers home the point that sinful behavior begins with thoughts in our minds. These thoughts function as suggestions or temptations. Hence, victory over sin requires engaging and attacking our thoughts—talking back to our thoughts—before they lead us to sin.

This means that the mind represents the front line of the spiritual battle. Surely, we can win many external battles through behavioral modification. Take, for example, a noteworthy practice from the legendary Billy Graham. The story has been told repeatedly that the venerable evangelist refused to meet alone with a woman other than one of his family members. On the surface, this practice looks good, one that surely minimizes the possibility of many forms of sin. It reminds me of the practice of curfew back when I was a teen. I can still hear my parents saying, "Nothing good happens after midnight." Or more to the point, "Keep your pants on." Such forms of behavioral modification surely have their place, especially for the young in the faith—but are they loving? Back to Graham: Does the Christian man love both the

---

2. Quoted in Evagrius, *Praktikos*, xix.

Lord and his female neighbor by refusing to meet her alone? Or does such a practice, in effect, represent a sin of omission or, more practically, hinder the spiritual or professional influence and advancement of women? Perhaps more importantly, does such a practice deprive men of edifying conversations or providential appointments with women, especially sisters in Christ?

I have discovered, however, that victories in outer spiritual warfare only get me so far in my goal of Christlikeness. In fact, they have led to legalism, a spiritually immature place fitting for infants and adolescents in the faith but far from the spiritual freedom I have been promised by Christ through the Spirit. They also led me to a pharisaic preoccupation with position and posture, and to a neglect of my interior person. In other words, I found it easier to do Christianity than to be Christlike. This explains, in part, why I found the teaching of Evagrius so helpful. In short, he identifies eight categories of thoughts or suggestions—he calls them *logismoi*—which tempt us away from love for God and neighbor. He then offers a weapon by which to combat these suggestions: *antirrhêtikos* or *talking back*. More specifically, he encourages Christians to talk back to specific temptations with specific passages of Scripture. Evagrius even provides a catalog of Scripture passages for us by Christ-followers.

Personally, I have found this weapon to be a great addition to the arsenal. I like that it harkens back to Jesus' impressive victory over Satan in the wilderness, where he talked back and defeated each temptation with the Word of God. It finds support among spiritual directors and counselors as an effective form of cognitive behavioral therapy, a prescription for healing from anxiety, eating disorders, and much more. It encourages immersion into and memorization of the Scriptures so we are ready to face the *logismoi* as they arise. Plus, it is best done in small groups where Christ-followers may discern their thoughts together and offer one another biblical talking-back points. Finally, it harmonizes well with other spiritual disciplines, such as prayer, fasting, giving, service, silence, and solitude.

I hope you, the reader, find relevance in Evagrius, as well as the broader desert tradition. While we are separated by thousands of years, the desert *abbas* and *ammas* (fathers and mothers) wrestled with many of the same issues we wrestle with. Like us, they struggled with temptation from within and without. They battled both inner and external forces in their attempt to more often choose virtue rather than vice. They did not do so to "earn their salvation," the generic critique by Protestants of anything remotely Catholic (or Orthodox). Instead, motivated by love for God and neighbor, as well as empowered by the Holy Spirit, they worked out their salvation in response to the invitation of Jesus to "Follow me." While they worked out their faith

in the desert, the spiritual practices they employed towards spiritual transformation transfer easily into the modern context.

One final note: This book has been written and rewritten amid massive tumult and transformation in the social and political landscape of the
United States, including such movements as #MeToo, Black Lives Matter,
the COVID-19 pandemic, and George Floyd and Breonna Taylor protests.
While this modest work does not address American politics as such, the
insights of the desert fathers remain relevant. Why? Because as we make
progress in discipleship and more fully order our interior lives, we likewise
can grow in our capacity to recognize and disentangle ourselves from the
durable systems and scripts of sin in society—including gender, class, and
racial inequalities.

Acknowledgments

We, the authors, are historians. Hence, most of our "best friends" are dead, but we still desire to acknowledge that we stand on their intellectual shoulders. Most notably, working backwards chronologically, we thank the American Evangelical tradition, the Puritans, the Anabaptists, the German Pietists, the Reformers, the Roman tradition (especially that of vices and virtues), the Orthodox tradition (especially hesychasm), and the desert tradition. The criticisms we have leveled at Evangelicalism should be viewed as the faithful wounds of a friend (Prov 27:6). Among the living, we thank those who helped us along, including Rebecca Konyndyk DeYoung, Angela Tilby, David Brakke, and others. Finally, we acknowledge the incredible love and support of Valerie Cocar and Debbie Hamstra, without whom this project would have faltered from the outset.

Introduction

SAM HAMSTRA JR. WITH SAMUEL COCAR

Over twenty years ago, David Wells, one of the leading voices among American Evangelicals, wrote these words:

> It is one thing to understand what Christ's deliverance means; it is quite another to see this worked out in life with depth and reality, to see its moral splendor. It is one thing to know the Gospel; it is quite another to see it lived. That is when its truth catches fire in the imagination. That is what makes the Gospel so attractive. The evangelical Church today, with some exceptions, is not very inspiring in this regard. It is not being heroic. It is exhibiting too little of the moral splendor that Christ calls it to exhibit . . . It is mostly empty of real moral vision, and without a recovery of that vision its faith will soon disintegrate.[1]

Not much has changed since 1998 when Wells penned that scathing critique of American Evangelicalism.

We write this treatise at a time when American Evangelicalism, of which we are a part, looks more like the unfaithful wife of Hosea than the holy bride and faithful body of Christ. Perhaps this is as it has always been for this particular segment of Christianity, save for specific manifestations. We believe that our most recent promiscuity reveals itself most prominently in an undisciplined life. Too often we talk about following Christ but fail to practice the spiritual disciplines practiced by Jesus and recorded for us in the inspired Word of God. We treat long evenings of prayer and multiple

---

1. Wells, *Losing Our Virtue*, 180.

1

days of fasting as ancient practices with no practical use in modernity. We can't imagine days of silence and solitude in the wilderness—or even one day without our phones. And let's not even talk about tithing, lest we all sink into the depths of guilt.

As Evangelicals, we embrace the salutary role of spiritual disciplines. With the late Donald Bloesch, we recognize that while "spiritual disciplines do not make reparation for sin, nor do they merit grace, which is always undeserved," they are "necessary to help us live out the implications of our faith in the world."[2] Yet, as national surveys reveal, we readily forsake even one of the easiest and, coincidently, thickest of the corporate disciplines: weekly attendance at worship services, where we hear the Word of God proclaimed, receive the Lord's Supper, renew our covenant with the Lord, and encourage one another through prayer and testimony. The end result of this undisciplined life, so it seems to us, is a gnostic-like religion that separates justification from sanctification, divorces talk from walk, ideas from action, and faith from obedience. This modern version of the Evangelical faith has seemingly conveniently neglected the biblical truth that:

> [Spiritual] renewal is not limited to God's justifying judgment. Something must precede and follow God's acquittal. Something happens to us, and for us. What precedes may be put under the heading of guilt and repentance; what follows may be labeled transformation and persistence.[3]

In short, we are not being "transformed from one degree of glory to another" (2 Cor 3:18), and it does not seem to bother us.

The undisciplined life of which we speak flows naturally from the way we think. As a result of an emphasis on the justification of the ungodly by faith, which is itself often cast as nothing more than intellectual assent to doctrine, we "view as optional the kind of heartfelt trust and confidence in the Lord that makes the salvation of Christ effectual in (our) lives."[4] In other words, we fail to embrace the integral relationship between salvation and the life of devotion, to recognize "that the life of devotion is the battleground on which our salvation is fought for and continually recovered," to commit ourselves to working out or appropriating our salvation in faith and love by the power of the Spirit within us (Phil 2:2).[5]

---

2. Bloesch, *Holy Spirit*, 323.

3. Van der Kooi and van den Brink, *Christian Dogmatics*, 651.

4. Bloesch, *Crisis of Piety*, 16.

5. Bloesch, *Crisis of Piety*, 16.

But there is more about the way we think that has contributed to our undisciplined life. We have, by and large, failed to take seriously the biblical message of two kingdoms, with all that it implies. The Scriptures are clear. Two kingdoms, one of light and the other of darkness, one of God and the other demonic, are locked in irrevocable warfare.[6] Furthermore, this world, while good, is the battleground on which the two kingdoms contend. In fact, "our Father's world" has been subjugated by the "god of this world" (Eph 2:2), the "prince of the power of the air" (2 Cor 4:4), the "prince of this world" (John 14:30). But there will come the riposte: surely Satan has been dethroned, even mortally wounded, by the death and resurrection of Christ. We reply that Christ has won the war but the enemy has not been vanquished. Christ is King of Kings, but demonic powers continue to wage battle against his rule, harassing even believers. As Christ-followers, then, who have submitted to the sovereign reign of Christ, have enlisted in his army, and serve as his soldiers, we live under constant attack from destructive and demonic forces. Each day we rise up, put on the armor of God (Eph 6:11), and enter the spiritual battlefield. This combat takes place, first and foremost, in our minds, while we live in the good but broken world God created as the theater for his glory. Joyce Meyer states this reality as forcefully and clearly as anyone:

> We are engaged in a war. Our enemy is Satan. The mind is the battlefield. The devil works diligently to set up strongholds in our mind. He does it through strategy and deceit, through well-laid plans and deliberate deception. He is in no hurry; he takes his time to work out his plan. Thoughts are the key—"As you think so you are" (Prov. 23:7).[7]

A failure to take seriously the biblical concept of the kingdom of darkness leads to nothing less than ignominious defeat. In contrast, when we recognize and respect it, we embrace with enthusiasm the disciplined life.

Closely related to our amnesia about two kingdoms is a cozy and confusing relationship with the world. Tim Keller, among others, notes that when Western culture began to change dramatically in the middle of the twentieth century, culture became a problem the American church could not ignore. As the cardinal cultural institutions stopped supporting Christianity, many Christians felt out of place in their own society. Keller writes, "The reasons for the culture shift continue to be a subject of much debate,

6. See Boyd, *God at War.*
7. Meyer, *Battlefield of the Mind.*

but one thing is certain: it became increasingly harder for evangelical Christians to be indifferent to culture."[8] Keller continues:

> During the greater part of the twentieth century, American evangelicals were indifferent to culture, focusing on conversions. More recently many American evangelical Christians have abandoned that pietistic stance. One of several reasons is that such a stance is naive about the culture's role in discipleship. The reality is that if the church does not think much about culture—about what parts are good, bad, or indifferent according to the Bible—its members will begin to uncritically imbibe in the values of culture. They will become assimilated to culture, despite intentions to the contrary. . . . If we are not deliberately thinking about culture, we will simply be confirmed to it without ever knowing it is happening.[9]

One would be hard pressed to prove that such is not currently the case. As citizens of heaven and residents on earth, we seek to live out our faith in the world while at the same time loving the Lord who stands against the world.[10] In the process, however, we often fail to take on the difficult work of discernment and are therefore seduced by "the prince of this world," who bends and even perverts for his own ends that which is good in the world. Observe, for example, our propensity to refer to the world as a mission field rather than a battlefield. That subtle yet significant preference frames the world as a place of opportunity rather than one of struggle, even defeat. It encourages us to lower our guard or take off our armor. Consequently, we become acclimated to the culture of the world and confuse cultural norms for biblical truths and efficient practices for virtuous ones. Our cultural accommodation is so extensive that story after story and survey after survey documents that the lives of Christ-followers, both corporately and individually, differ little from those who have no place for him.[11]

Surely, we have been "led astray from sincere and pure devotion to Christ" (2 Cor 11:3). What our fellowship needs—first and foremost—is consecration to God, who has revealed himself to us in Jesus Christ. Over fifty years ago, Donald Bloesch offered a similar call, one whose words ring true to this day:

8. Keller, *Center Church*, 184.

9. Keller, *Center Church*, 185–86.

10. The Gospel of John uses "world" (Gk. *kosmos*) in different senses. Contextually, it may refer to the sum total of humankind (whom YHWH loves) or to the civilizational systems of human power and control that stand in opposition to divine authority.

11. For a quantitative grounding, we might look to similar rates of marital infidelity and divorce between Christians and non-Christians.

When Christians again place their fear and trust in the living God; when they seek to draw close to the spiritual wellsprings of the faith in prayer and devotion; when they seek to imitate their Savior in a life of outgoing loving service to others, then the secular age will pay heed to their gospel, and perhaps once more God will become meaningful to men (and women). An age that has experienced the death of God needs now to experience the power of the resurrection of His Son in the lives of believers. And the remnant of the faithful need to be filled and empowered by the Spirit of God so that they can give an intelligible and compelling witness to a world groping in the darkness of sin and plagued by the anxiety of meaninglessness.[12]

Our motivation for such a disciplined life and its corollary, holy living, is "not some abstract categorical imperative," but love for our triune God, a love that glorifies the Father as we become more like Christ through the power of the Holy Spirit at work within us.[13] Gregory of Nazianzus once wrote

I share everything with Christ, spirit and body, nails and resurrection. Christ . . . thou are for me my native land, my strength, my glory, everything. Christ is my strength and my breath and the wonderful prize for my running. It is he who enables me to run well. I love him as my purest love because for those whom he loves he is faithful beyond all that we can conceive. In him is my joy ever if he chooses to send me some suffering, because I aspire to be purified as gold in the fire.[14]

To that end, we look for guides who can present to us their hard-fought experience in the way of Jesus. As Olivier Clément notes, "To climb a mountain it is not enough to have a map; a guide is necessary."[15] There are many options, but we surely find such guides in the desert fathers and mothers—men and women, soldiers of Christ, who retreated to the deserts of Egypt, Syria, and Palestine in the fourth and fifth centuries to become living martyrs and to seek a union with God and Christ they could not find elsewhere. To be sure, they are not the interlocutors with whom contemporary Evangelicals most prefer to interact, names such as Calvin, Edwards,

12. Bloesch, *Crisis of Piety*, 18.

13. Bloesch, *Crisis of Piety*, 18.

14. Thank you to Olivier Clément, author of *The Roots of Christian Mysticism*, for pointing us to this poem by Gregory, which may be found in his *Theological Poems* (PG 37:623–24).

15. Clément, *Roots of Christian Mysticism*, 145.

Barth, or Lewis. But they offer us invaluable wisdom on disciplines of devotion, the cultivation of virtue, the destruction of vice, and role of the body in spiritual formation and warfare. We ignore their insights at our peril.

The structure of this book flows from the general to the specific. Chapter 1 provides a rudimentary summary of both the Gospel and human nature. We do so to provide the conceptual map on which to locate our book, one that addresses the disciplined life required for victory in our spiritual battle to become more like Christ. If we hope as Christians to experience victory, we best possess accurate knowledge of our enemy—temptation, which gives birth to sin. In chapter 2, then, we examine what it means to miss the mark, as well as the inevitable corollary of righteousness, the shape of human life conformed to the divine will—for both the glory of the triune God and the flourishing of humankind. In chapter 3, after a brief discussion on virtues and vices, we point readers to a framework found in the writings of the church fathers, as well as the writings of the desert mothers (ammas) and fathers (abbas). This framework is the *logismoi*—eight categories of the thoughts or suggestions which function as temptations for monks, as well as ordinary Christians, seeking a virtuous life. We then introduce the spiritual discipline or weapon of *antirrhêtikos* or *talking back*.

Chapter 5 suggests that the key to victory on the spiritual battlefield is a disciplined life, a life of devotion characterized by the regular and effective use of an arsenal of spiritual weapons. To further our case, we discuss the gaps currently present in the spiritual practices of modern Evangelicalism, gaps that discourage a whole-hearted embrace of a disciplined life and spiritual practices (weapons). Chapter 6 proposes a foundational spirituality or core triad of prayer, fasting, and giving as fundamental and essential for every Christ-follower.

Chapter 7 is the heart and soul of this book. We begin it with the assumption that we who have been saved by grace through faith desire to love the Lord our God with heart, soul, mind, and strength, and to love our neighbor as we love ourselves. Motivated by love, we seek to become more and more like Christ, our Savior and Lord, by modeling the fruit of the Spirit with our lives. Motivated by that same love, we have responded to the call of Christ to serve him through a variety of vocations. Not long after entering the road of discipleship, we discover, like Paul, that we do what we don't want to do and don't do what we want to do. Our experiences of being unfaithful help us discover typical sins or vices. With the help of Evagrius, we will categorize them as gluttony or hoarding, lust or impurity, avarice or greed, anger, sadness or dejection, acedia or listlessness, vainglory or vanity, and pride. Then we will recommend putting to use our primary weapon—our sword, the Word of God (Eph 6:17). With his help, we also learn how to nip temptation in the bud by quoting specific Scripture passages back at it.

After an excursus illuminating one of the more important and influential individuals in the history of the Christian church—Maximus Confessor—we provide examples of *talking back* from the desert tradition. In this chapter, we allow the anecdotes and counsels of the monks to speak largely for themselves.

Here are a few logistical items. First, below the title of each section or chapter of this volume, you will find an ascription of authorship. These acknowledgements follow standard practice. Samuel Cocar with Sam Hamstra, for example, is meant to convey that Cocar was the primary author and I contributed secondarily, and vice versa. Second, we have strategically utilized a variety of translations for the numerous references to Scripture in this volume. For those instances in which we do not note the translation, the reader may assume the New International Version. Third, although we have done our best to represent careful scholarship, this work is not an academic monograph on patristics. It does not argue the finer points of Evagrius in Greek and Latin recensions; rather, we attempt in some small way to cut a channel between the pastoral wisdom of the desert fathers and modern disciples, who so desperately need it. We are indebted to a variety of theologians, historians, and patrologists, and we have attempted to give credit where credit is due throughout the volume.

So, let us begin.

Chapter 1

Our Spiritual Battle to Become Like Christ

SAMUEL COCAR WITH SAM HAMSTRA JR.

We, like you, self-identify as Christians. We, like you, are among those who have decided to follow Jesus and who have been incorporated into his church by baptism. Together, we—reader and writers—are united as one body by one Spirit, with one hope, Lord, faith, baptism, and God and Father of all (Eph 4:4–5). Together we identify ourselves as a chosen people, holy nation, royal priesthood, and God's prized possession. Together we embrace a two-thousand-year history characterized by grace and gore, courage and cowardice, saints and sinners, faithfulness and betrayal, memorable moments and others we wish we could forget. At times we have lived as a faithful bride awaiting her groom, but at other times we have been nothing less than the faithless, promiscuous wife of Hosea. Still we press on, seeking to love the Lord, both individually and corporately, with heart, soul, mind, and strength, while also seeking to love our neighbor, without which we cannot fulfill our first love.

As human beings, each one of us represents a unique mixture of cognitive, emotive, and volitional elements or, as a popular typology goes: head, heart, and hands. Some of us are heady and our decision to follow

Christ represents the fruit of an intellectual inquiry; we were and remain convinced that Jesus is who he claimed to be and that the atonement theory of the gospel makes sense. Some of us are more emotive; our decision to follow Christ represents a loving response to the love of God for us. Messages, movies, and music about the Lord touched our hearts and prompted commitment to the one who has chosen to adopt us as his own. The rest of us are more action oriented. Following the example of the apostles on the Sea of Galilee, when Jesus called, we responded. It didn't make sense and it wasn't prompted by emotion. We just trusted and obeyed. For many of us action-oriented disciples, the call from Jesus came through the voices of our parents, who raised us in the way of the Lord, or through the church to which our parents belonged. For others, like Saul who became Paul, the call came more mysteriously. No matter who voiced the call, the response was a decision to follow.

Unlike all other mammals, the nexus of our personhood is our soul or heart, a reality that reflects the image of God, thereby allowing us freedom to create, cooperate, and communicate with one another and with the Lord. Without the soul, we are nothing more than animals; with the soul, we are either enemies of God (Rom 5:10) or children and friends of God (Gal 3:26). We have discovered over time, like many before us, that the soul, the essence of our being, is restless until it finds rest in God. Augustine may be credited with voicing that reality, but every Christian has known it to be true. We long for fellowship with the Lord and, as human beings, have the freedom to seek it through spiritual personal disciplines: prayer, solitude, and corporate disciplines, like participation in our congregation's weekly (perhaps even daily) gathering.

The freedom of which we speak, as human beings created in the image of God, brings about a necessity that does not exist for the animal. Here we draw on the excellent work of the late Romano Guardini, who, by reason of his influence upon the last two popes of the Roman Catholic Church, may be safely described as one of the more significant Christians of the twentieth century. In his *Learning the Virtues that Lead to God*, Guardini asks, "How does a healthy animal grow and develop?" His answer: "By following its urges." When an animal follows its urges, everything goes well. The animal eats until it is satisfied and no more. The animal sleeps until it is rested, no more. When the urge for procreation is active, the animal follows it. "The manner, the type, so to speak, according to which the life of nature is carried on is simply that of working out its fulfillment. The interior drive expresses itself in external action."[1]

---

1. Guardini, *Learning the Virtues*, 86. This work was originally published in 1963.

In contrast, observes Guardini, what we may refer to as an urge operates differently in humans. First, thinking about the urge intensifies the urge. No animal, for example, "follows the drive toward food as much as a [person] who makes the pleasure its own and thereby harms (him or her) self." Second, the urges of animals are bound, secure, and regulated, while those of human beings may become unregulated and their meaning endangered.[2] This means that we have a unique freedom to our life impulses, but that freedom brings about a necessity that does not exist for the animal: that is, "the need to keep our urges in an order which is freely willed and to overcome our tendency toward excess or toward a wrong direction."[3] What Guardini helps us see is that the need for disciplined lives flows from human impulses "basic to self-preservation and self-development." Guardini writes:

> The building up of what we call "the personality," its preservation in the world, and its activity and creativity is based upon mental and spiritual urges. There is the urge toward recognition and esteem, toward power in all its forms. There is the urge toward social and community life, toward freedom and culture, toward knowledge and artistic creation. All of these urges have, as we said, their significance as impulses basic to self-preservation and self-development. But they are also inclined to become excessive, to bring our life out of harmony with the lives of others and so to become disturbing or destructive. Therefore, a constant discipline is necessary, a discipline whose principles are determined by ethics and practical philosophy; this discipline is asceticism.[4]

As Christ-followers, we begin the disciplined life by following the example of Jesus Christ. Like him, we long to love the Lord and love our neighbors. A review of the four Gospels reveals that Jesus modeled a three-dimensional life, one we may summarize as up, in, and out. In Luke 6:12, for example, we read that Jesus went out to a mountain where he spent an entire evening in conversation (prayer) with his Father in heaven. When the morning came, he gathered with his disciples and chose from them twelve whom he named apostles (6:13). Then he approached a great multitude of people who came to hear him and be healed by him (6:18). Like Jesus, we seek to embody this three-dimensional life by spending private time with the Lord, fellowshipping with fellow brothers and sisters in Christ, and serving the needy in our communities. Today it has become popular to suggest

2. Guardini, *Learning the Virtues*, 87.

3. Guardini, *Learning the Virtues*, 88.

4. Guardini, *Learning the Virtues*, 89–90.

that we need to balance each of these three dimensions, but perhaps exact balance need not concern us unduly. Some of us are contemplatives and others activists. Some of us are introverts (and prefer fellowship with dead authors) and others extroverts. Yet each of us, like Jesus, will benefit from some measure of up, in, and out.

As Christians, we also desire to discover and embody the teaching of Jesus. So we spend time in the Bible, the written Word of God. Both private-ly and corporately, we read, study, memorize, and meditate on God's Word. But no matter how hard we look, we will not find in the Bible a systematic catechism composed of questions and answers about how we should live; that would come later. Neither do we find a one-size-fits-all manual. Some are called to hate their parents, while others are told to care for them. Some are encouraged to sell their possessions and others to keep them. What is good for you, then, is not necessarily good for me. In one anecdote of the Christian desert, we read that a brother asked Abba Nesteros what the for-mer needed to do to attain perfection. The abba responded that Abraham was hospitable, and God was with him; Elijah loved quiet, and God was with him; David was humble, and God was with him. However our heart draws us toward the will of God, we can follow it and be at peace.[5]

While the Bible does not provide a universal template for disciple-ship, it does offer the teaching of Jesus through four Gospels and offers that teaching within a grand narrative, with the Old Testament serving as the beginning of the story and the remainder of the New Testament as its conclusion. By this design, then, we understand that the Gospels are to be interpreted within the whole of Scripture. This, of course, leads to more reading, studying, memorizing, and meditating.

While the interpretation of the Gospels varies in time and place, we can be sure of this: as Christ-followers we are to become like Jesus. This invita-tion to *being* like Jesus clearly involves growing in the grace and knowledge of the Lord (2 Pet 3:18), but it does not end there. It also involves developing the very character of Christ, commonly referred to as the fruit of the Spirit (Gal 5:22–23) and approximating the sinless life of Christ. In short, we are to be holy (1 Pet 1:15–16). Of course, that is easier said than done. Each one of us is a distinctive but fallen human being created in the image of God for fellowship with God. We are also both sinners and sinful. Like the apostle Paul, we do what we don't want to do and fail to do what we want to do (Rom 7:15). In other words, we sin by commission and omission—and we do so more times than we can count, because our soul has been contami-nated by sin. Left to our own devices, even the most educated and civilized

5. Waddell, trans., ed., *Desert Fathers*, 68.

among us succumb to temptation. It comes naturally, beginning with our thoughts, which develop into intentions before taking shape in behavior.

Furthermore, we live in a world characterized by evil and inhabited by the devil. Merrill Unger was on the right track when he averred, in his 1977 book *What Demons Can Do to Saints*, that we can be harassed by evil spirits. Unger showed that "demon possession" is too fraught a phrase and opted, instead, for a spectrum of demonization. In the spiritual ecology of the desert, all of us who name Christ as Lord are thus harassed. We all have stray thoughts and unsanctified emotions and dispositions which constitute the stuff of spiritual warfare (and, of course, also discipleship or formation).[6] Martin Luther voiced this reality in his popular hymn "*Ein feste Burg ist unser Gott.*" The English translation falls short of the original but makes clear our reality: "This world, with devils filled, threatens to undo us." In other words, while this is our Father's world and Jesus Christ is King of Kings and Lord of Lords, the devil and his minions have not yet laid down their arms. They continue to terrorize us through direct and indirect attacks, the latter taking shape in structures and ideologies. They continue to inhabit political and economic strongholds from which they attack us. And they do so even within our ranks—the church of Jesus Christ. To imagine spiritual warfare as a dimension of Christian knowledge and experience to be deployed secondarily or contingently—when we meet the demoniac yelling obscenities, breaking shackles, and gashing himself among the tombs (cf. Mark 5)—is to myopically and tragically misunderstand the biblical picture. In the Pauline cosmology, the world is a sphere roiling with activity of a personal and incorporeal nature.

So, here we are: Christ-followers who face constant resistance, from within and without, to our efforts to become like Jesus. The biblical writers describe our predicament as nothing less than war (2 Cor 10:3), an image that implies winners and losers, conquests and casualties, victories and defeats, as well weapons and armor, toil and endurance. These images encourage us to put on the full armor of God (Eph 6:10–20), employ the weapons at our disposal (2 Cor 10:4–5), and fight the good fight (1 Tim 6:12). We do so with hope, for God the Father, who loved us before the foundation of the world, sent his Son to redeem us from our sin and also sent the Holy Spirit to sanctify us. We know the Father will protect us from being tempted beyond our capacity to deal with it (1 Cor 10:13). We also know the power of the Spirit within us is greater than any power in the world (1 John 4:4). We may likewise hold out hope for developing the character of Christ and becoming like Christ.

6. Unger, *What Demons Can Do to Saints*.

This admittedly cursory summary of both the gospel and human nature provides the map on which we may locate this book. The arsenal or spiritual toolbox described herein represents the disciplined life required for victory in our spiritual battle to become more like Christ. That is, in this volume we describe some of the weapons employed by the Christ-follower to win the battle. In the process, we draw from the writings of the desert mothers and fathers, a tradition disparaged by earlier Protestants and largely unknown to modern Protestants, but one beneficial for all Protestants. David G. R. Keller writes,

> Like us, the desert fathers and mothers came from all walks of life with names like Mary, John the Dwarf, and Moses the Robber. Like us, they sought spiritual transformation through an experience of God in prayer. Like us they were influenced by popular ways of life in secular society (*politeia*). Like us they recognized that the inhabited world may distract Christians from a deep personal longing for God. Like us they discovered the need for physical separation from usual patterns of life. Like us they are ascetics who, like Jesus, adopted a way of life characterized by discipline and practice.[7]

This stream of knowledge shares some tributaries with the Greco-Roman classical tradition, which constituted much of the soil of the Christian movement from the end of the first century onward. We have the most visible affinity for the tradition called Aristotelian. In the classical tradition, one seeks first and foremost not a set of correct positions (i.e., orthodoxy), but rather to be a certain kind of person, one characterized by the possession and ongoing cultivation of certain virtues. These virtues are considered *aretai*, "excellences," because they collectively represent the zenith of personal and social formation—what it means to become like Christ.

Of course, we are generalizing to some degree, but fairly. We do not want to run roughshod over the variations in Greco-Roman philosophies. Surely, we will see variations in the principal virtues between Epicureanism and Stoicism, between the Aristotelian tradition and the Platonic. But the formation and refinement of the human person was integral to them all. This sort of overall orientation to life is strongly attested by, for instance, the Stoic philosopher Epictetus. Consider this excerpt from *The Art of Living*, rendered in the fresh translation of Sharon Lebell:

> On the occasion of an accidental event, don't just react in a haphazard fashion: Remember to turn inward and ask what

---

7. Keller, *Oasis of Wisdom*, xv.

resources you have for dealing with it. Dig deeply. You possess strengths you might not realize you have. Find the right one. Use it. If you encounter an attractive person, then self-restraint is the resource needed; if pain or weakness, then stamina; if verbal abuse, then patience. As time goes by and you build on the habit of matching the appropriate inner resource to each incident, you will not tend to get carried away by life's appearances. You will stop feeling overwhelmed so much of the time.[8]

We could just as easily cite the *Meditations* of Marcus Aurelius or the sometimes-vexing *Republic* of Plato. Although the latter has very specific views on the arrangement of the ideal society, the perfection of the human person remains central.

While drawing from patristic traditions, we seek to avoid the crucial mistake of dividing the spiritual battle into two separate parts: preparation and participation, or spiritual formation and spiritual warfare. While it may have served some purpose in the past, those distinctions obscure the reality that the moment we prepare for battle we enter the battle; there is no safe zone. Like Jesus, and countless monks who years later followed his example, we may withdraw from the world to the wilderness to pray, but even there we will be tempted by Satan. In the desert, we find God and we fight demons. Hence, at all times and all places each person who names Christ as Lord wrestles not only with his or her very own flesh and blood, but also "against the cosmic powers over this present darkness, against the spiritual forces of evil in the heavenly places" (Eph 6:12). In short, when we seek to be formed into the likeness of Christ we simultaneously engage in war.[9]

We also seek to avoid the error of placing information above transformation, the defense of intellectual tenets above the cultivation of the virtuous life, orthodoxy over orthopraxis. Countless modern disciples of Jesus have fallen into the trap of thinking that once they've hammered out the correct ideological position their Christian homework is finished. For them, moral improvement is a part of the Christian life, but the central theater is

---

8. Epictetus, *Art of Living*, 17.

9. It is our hope that theology in the future will lead to the erasure of the conceptual division between spiritual formation and spiritual warfare. While it may have served some purpose, that edifice has also complicated and obscured. For the desert fathers, the spiritual masters of yesteryear, being found in Christ and being formed in Christ meant waging a perpetual battle with forces—infernal and atmospheric—which intend constantly to disrupt our union with God, shake our confidence, and corrupt our modest virtues. Stated theologically: both regeneration and sanctification necessarily entail mortification. To employ a financial analogy: asset protection is part of the same domain of activity and concern as wealth generation. And the follower of Jesus is wealthy indeed.

their *worldview*. All stripes of Christians, whether mainline, confessional, or Evangelical, have sometimes succumbed to the temptation of placing correct position over proper personhood. To clarify: Christians have become largely content with endorsing the right positions on various issues. Abortion is wrong. Homosexuality is wrong. Or both are *right*. Gun ownership is a constitutional right, or it's a national plague. And so on.

As an alternative to both of those errors, we affirm the link between spiritual formation and spiritual warfare, and between the disciplined life and the life of devotion. We also commit ourselves to using each of the resources at our disposal to achieve the treasure of a Christlike character. It is to these ends that we have written the present work. Our goal is to have produced a work that fraternally binds practical, spiritual, and systematic theology. We have sought to produce neither a dogmatic theology of sin—a hamartiology for purists—nor a simple grab bag of spiritual practices and disciplines, without critical reflection on their place in the spiritual life and progress of Christ-followers. Rather, our intent has been to produce a treatise which integrates biblical and theological perspectives on the spiritual life with the proper gear for the trek. We have reserved the right to draw insights from every branch of the Christian tradition, but have deferred to ancient sources over modern, to the patristic and apostolic over the sectarian and parochial. We do this with the hope that this book will help the reader along the path to becoming a more conscious pilgrim, a more fruitful servant, and a fiercer soldier.

We do so with the conviction that, for the apostle Paul, the world is a sphere pervaded by activity of a personal and ethereal nature. These are the elementary spirits with whom we battle. Paul reminds us in Ephesians 6:12, "For we do not wrestle against flesh and blood, but against the rulers, against the authorities, against the cosmic powers over this present darkness, against the spiritual forces of evil in the heavenly places" (ESV). That Christians are still engaged with flesh-and-blood enemies can be considered nothing other than a tragedy. The answer to Kay Arthur's question "Lord, is it warfare?" is always "Yes." Does your mind wander when you pray? (Remember that that the Lord Jesus considered one hour to be a short watch with Peter, James, and John). An elder *abba* would identify this tendency as perhaps a spirit of lethargy, and thus spiritual warfare—and he would give you a concrete, disciplinarian remedy. This is the tradition, the sort of knowledge, which we want Evangelicals to claim and recover. Theological precision is no trifle, but we ought to strive more ardently for that holiness without which no one will see the Lord (Heb 12:14).

Chapter 2

This World with Devils Filled

A Biblical Survey of Sin

SAMUEL COCAR WITH SAM HAMSTRA JR.

It is said that if you know your enemy and know yourself, you will not be imperiled in a hundred battles.

—Sun Tzu

If we hope as Christians to please the Lord with the fruit of our lives, to be good soldiers of Christ, we had best possess accurate knowledge of our enemy—*sin*. In our day and age, it feels almost embarrassing to reify sin. We don't like talking about it. We would much sooner, and more comfortably, abandon biblical and theological terms in order to speak of imperfections, psychological guilt, brokenness, or "mistakes" (which Peter O'Toole's Henry II famously claimed were worse). In the biblical record, however, sin seems to constitute its own character. It is a living monster, a parasite to the human will, a malicious microbe in a hundred different strains.

Studying our enemy, however, does not translate to an unbroken, macabre meditation on the ugliness of human evil. As we examine what it means to miss the mark, we cannot help but see the mark: the character of God. The inevitable corollary of studying sin is studying righteousness, the shape of human life conformed to the divine will—for both the glory of the triune God and the flourishing of humankind. With this in mind, we begin our study of sin with the familiar narrative of the first family of humankind.[1]

ADAM, EVE, AND THE ANTEDILUVIAN WORLD

After God formed the earth, its animals and vegetation, he created human beings, male and female, in his own image (Gen 1:27). We often refer to the following verses as the creational mandate. God enters a covenant with Adam and Eve (who will not be named until Gen 3:20). In it they receive responsibilities as well as privileges with regard to nonhuman creation:

> God blessed them and said to them, "Be fruitful and multiply! Fill the earth and subdue it! Rule over the fish of the sea and the birds of the air and every creature that moves on the ground." Then God said, "I now give you every seed-bearing plant on the face of the entire earth and every tree that has fruit with seed in it. They will be yours for food." (1:28–29, NET)

Adam, charged by God as the steward of the garden of Eden, receives from him a single command. God allows Adam to eat from any tree in the garden, except the tree of the knowledge of good and evil. He assures Adam that the day he eats from it would also be the day of his death (2:16–17).

Adam, however, does not long enjoy the paradise maintained by his simple obedience. After articulating the terms of their covenant with God (3:2–3), Eve gives in to the subtle reasoning of the serpent. The serpent's argument for eating the fruit becomes Eve's personal rationalization:

> Then the woman saw that the tree was good for food and delightful to look at, and that it was desirable for obtaining wisdom. So, she took some of its fruit and ate it; she also gave some to her husband, who was with her, and he ate it. (3:6, Holman Christian Standard Bible)

The effects are immediate. Adam and Eve understand that they are naked and sew fig leaves together to alleviate their shame. God then questions

---

1. We are aware of varying perspectives on the genre and historicity of Genesis, especially chapters 1 and 2. The reader is encouraged to integrate textual and theological convictions into the account that follows. See also the distinction between "Adam I" and "Adam II" in Brooks, *Road to Character*, xi.

the couple about their misconduct, at which point the man blames his wife (3:12) and Eve blames the wily serpent (3:13).

Paradise has been shattered. God curses the serpent, placing perpetual enmity between it and humankind (3:14–15). God then introduces increased labor pains and marital subordination to the woman (3:16), toil and futility to the man (3:18). Both must reckon with the inevitability of physical death (3:19).[2] Lastly, the couple are banished from the garden—an exile enforced by the presence of a formidably armed angelic guardian (3:23–24).

The first family continues to grow outside of Eden, but the ravaging effects of sin follow them. Adam and Eve's sons, Cain and Abel, both present offerings to the Lord. While God is pleased with the firstborn of Abel's flocks, he does not regard Cain's offering of produce (4:4–5). This renders Cain furious and downcast. The Lord's reply, however, is encouraging:

> Then the LORD said to Cain, "Why are you furious? And why are you downcast? If you do right, won't you be accepted? But if you do not do right, sin is crouching at the door. Its desire is for you, but you must master it. (4:6, HCSB)

The Lord gives Cain the opportunity to amend both his sacrifice and his disposition, without fear of wrath or repercussion. He also identifies the crossroads at which Cain has found himself: he must either master his sin or be vanquished by it.

That conversation has little effect on Cain and he promptly submits fully to his anger. Having invited his brother Abel to a secluded field, Cain murders him in cold blood (4:8). God is outraged and condemns Cain with a twofold curse: the ground will no longer yield a crop (reinforcing the curse on Adam) and Cain will be a restless wanderer (4:12). After Cain receives a mysterious mark which will preserve his life among the people he encounters, God once again drives Cain away from his presence (4:15–16).

Despite his divine punishment and gloomy prospects, Cain becomes integral to the advance of civilization. After he takes a wife, Cain builds a city and names it for his son Enoch (4:17). A few generations later, Cain's descendants become the patriarchs of important advancements in culture: nomadic herding, the playing of lyre and flute, and the crafting of tools in bronze and iron (4:20–22). Spiritually, there is a glimmer of hope in that "people began to call on the name of the Lord" around the time that

---

2. Evangelicals often spoke about "spiritual death," but more concretely, Adam and Eve are subjected to eventual mortality. The loss of communion with Elohim is apparent from the passage and does not require the spiritualizing gloss. Some early commentators have speculated that Adam was before this point neither definitively mortal nor immortal.

Seth—the son given in place of Abel—begins his family (4:26). Indeed, the legitimate line of Adam and Eve's descendants continues through Seth, not Cain (5:1). This line of "Sethites" includes patriarchs who live to incredible lifespans. We have no record of the spiritual legacy of these patriarchs, with the exception of Enoch (not Cain's son), who walked with God for three hundred years (Gen 5:21–24; cf. Heb 11:5).[3]

The spiritual tenor of the rest of civilization is contrastingly dismal. The "sons of God"—likely angelic beings—form unions with human women, producing physically giant warrior-heroes called Nephilim (Gen 6:1–4).[4] Evil pervades human society. The Lord perceives that "man's wickedness was widespread on the earth, and that every scheme his mind thought of was nothing but evil all the time" (6:5). Civilization seems to be universally violent and unjust (v. 11). Noah, who alone finds favor in God's eyes, is charged with carrying a remnant of the human and animal creation on a massive ark, thus becoming a new Adam after the earth is destroyed with water (6:17; 9:1–17).

In summary, the long golden age postulated in Greek mythology contrasts strongly to the paradise enjoyed by the original human family. The *shalom* of Eden is promptly shattered by the disobedience of Adam and Eve toward the single command of God. As humanity's representative, the consequences of their sin affect all who follow. Sin devastates the first family, as Cain, childishly disappointed over the inferiority of his sacrifice, murders his brother Abel.[5] The next few generations will see people beginning to call on the name of the Lord and advancing the arts of civilization and technology. Despite this, humankind still plunges headlong into violence and wickedness. God regrets his human creation and renders the slate clean by saving only Noah and his family from a universal flood.[6]

Jewish theology has posited the existence of "Noahide laws"—a code of seven moral mandates which God charged to Noah and his descendants. This code is alluded to in the book of *Jubilees* 7:20–28.[7] These hypothetical

3. There are many excellent modern editions of the pseudepigraphical *Book of Enoch* (*1 Enoch*). For a treatment of how *1 Enoch* sheds light on the cosmology and worldview of the NT authors, see Barker, *Lost Prophet*.

4. Of course, even if these beings are the product of intermarriage between Seth's line and Cain's line, as opposed to angelic-human union, moral chaos still reigns.

5. Jesus, alongside traditions in Jewish theology, endorses Abel as the first righteous martyr. See Matt 23:35, Luke 11:51.

6. The term used for the geographical extent of the flood is the ambiguous *eretz*, "land." More significant is that the flood was *anthropologically* universal. See 2 Pet 2:5.

7. The book of *Jubilees* is an ancient Jewish religious work of fifty chapters, considered one of the pseudepigrapha by Protestant, Roman Catholic, and Eastern Orthodox Churches. See English translation in Charles, trans., *Apocrypha and Pseudepigrapha*.

imperatives included prohibitions against theft, idolatry, and blasphemy, among others. As enticing as this hypothesis is, a formal, codified set of moral imperatives goes beyond the biblical record at this point. Humankind receives the indictment of being mentally focused on "nothing but evil all the time" (Gen 6:5), and of being extremely violent (Gen 6:14), as was apparent in the episodes of Cain and Lamech (Gen 4). We could easily ascribe pride, idolatry, as well as sexual immorality and promiscuity to the general charge of wickedness.[8]

FROM ABRAHAM THROUGH MOSES

As he did in the time of Noah, so in the time of Abram: God takes the initiative to fix that which is broken by sin. The appearance by God to Abram is an epic moment, as the transaction between God and Abraham marks the beginning of a particular covenant, one limited to a single family. It also teaches us, among other truths, that our sins and shortcomings place second to God's activity. Now, after the failed do-over with Noah, God takes a different approach, one hinted at in an earlier conversation with the serpent (Gen 3:15). He enters a covenant with Abram, one that promises a fourfold blessing of nationhood, a great name, divine protection, and the role of mediator of blessings—God will bless those who bless Abram and curse those who curse him. In return, God asks Abram to "go," pack up, and leave the known for the unknown, the relatively certain for the uncertain. Remarkably, Abraham obeys. The author of Hebrews later describes that action as faith: confidence in what we hope for and assurance about what we do not see (Heb 11:1). More importantly, the Abrahamic covenant clarifies the complexity of sin by linking faith to obedience. Abram's decision to leave home at God's invitation illustrates that the way to obedience is paved by faith in the promises of God.

In a short time, however, Abram also illustrates that the way of disobedience or sin is doubt in the promises of God. Shortly after leading Abram to the promised land, we learn that the patriarch decided to leave that land for a "foreign" land. There is no evidence of God's leading him to that decision. The lack of such portrays Abram as one stepping out on his own. We are left to conclude that Abram had faith sufficient to leave his first home for

---

8. If the apostle Paul's diatribe in Romans 1 can be applied to the antediluvian Gentile world, it also sheds some light on the extent of human depravity in general (see Rom 1:26–32). Paul indicates that these benighted Gentiles were guilty not of flouting a divinely proclaimed law (e.g., the Mosaic law), but rather of disobeying their internal consciences, which had the clear light of God's general revelation (Rom 1:18–25).

a new home but lacked faith to stay in his new home where he would have been blessed by God. The sin here appears innocent, but a lack of faith lies at its root. This shortcoming drives future decisions and establishes a recurring pattern of Abram trying to make a way for himself, a way that doesn't always include his wife, Sarai (Gen 12:11–13).

In addition, the failure of Abram in the face of presumed hostility or difficulty illustrates that sin is not primarily moralistic (a deviation from an external norm) or monistic (as related to our humanness) or religious (an offense against a cultic practice). It is relational and its cause is deep. While those who built the tower of Babel were motivated by pride, Abram's defection lies elsewhere. It lies in the fact that he does not cleave to the promises of God, and that leads to both unbelief and disobedience. As such, Abram's sin mirrors the disobedience of Adam and Eve and also foreshadows that of the seed of Abraham. Furthermore, the Abrahamic narratives affirm the deep-rootedness of sin, which cannot be eradicated even by heroic faith, much less by a flood.

That epic moment was followed by others, each involving an invitation by God to renew the covenant and reaffirm its fourfold promise. When Abram was ninety-nine years old, God asked Abram to seal the covenant by being the first of many to be circumcised. After this act of faithful obedience, God renamed the patriarch "father of many" or "Abraham," and his princess "Sarah," "matriarch." On another occasion, God called Abraham to sacrifice Isaac, his one and only son (Gen 22). Once again, Abraham, the one prone to making his own way, chose to trust God through obedience. The author of Hebrews once again connects obedience to faith in God's promises by stating that Abraham willingly sacrificed his son because he reasoned that God would bless him and make a nation of him by raising his son from death (Heb 11:17–19).

The relational or personal nature of sin dominates the patriarchal narratives as the children and grandchildren of Abraham follow in his footsteps, mirroring seasons of both faith and doubt, obedience and disobedience, righteousness and sin. Still, the nature of sin remains secondary to the primary story line of God's grace and faithfulness to a people bent on sin. Clearly, God will not allow his plan to miscarry. Time after time, he rescues it from human failure. This is especially prominent in God's plan to deliver his people from slavery in Egypt. The key figure in this narrative is Moses, a man introduced to us as both a murderer and one called by God to lead his people out of Egypt to the promised land. Moses dutifully fulfills his calling despite opposition from Egypt, the greatest military power in the ancient world, and despite the faithlessness and disobedience of the people of God. In the process, we see the Lord remembering his promises to Abraham (Exod 2:24; 3:6, 14–17; 6:2–8).

One of those promises was to make the seed of Abraham into a great nation. After the manifestation of his saving power at the Red Sea, God informed Moses that the time had come for the creation of a holy nation of believers (Exod 19:4–6). This people, the custodian of the ancient faith of Abraham and Sarah, would be joined together politically, socially, and spiritually through a covenant delivered by God to Moses at Sinai. The new theocracy included two types of law: apodictic and casuistic. The former, which includes the Decalogue, sets forth universal principles that are always binding and indisputable. The latter details specific cases and prescribes specific laws, statutes, and rules for the people of God. The Mosaic law, as Robin Routledge observes, "gave human beings an opportunity to play an active part in their relationship with God. It gave a choice: obey God's word and maintain the relationship or disobey and reject the relationship."[9] Once rejected, human beings require a mediator to both receive forgiveness and renew the relationship.

As with Abraham and his clan, sin within the theocracy is viewed as a fracture of a relationship through disobedience or rebellion against God's will. The Mosaic law, however, introduces two new elements which influence the history of redemption. The first is the notion of collective sin. Now that Israel is bound to God, they are responsible to God as both individuals and a nation. Consequently, we now witness collective sin in addition to individual sin. The story of the golden calf illustrates the reality of collective or national sin (Exod 32). While Moses spoke with God on Mount Sinai, the people of God grew fearful that their leader would not return. Unwilling to wait any longer, they encouraged Aaron to create gods to go before them. With no apparent resistance to the idea, Aaron gathered up the gold in the camp and fashioned it with a graving tool into a golden calf. It was about this time that God started a new conversation with Moses by describing the activities of "your people, whom you brought out of Egypt" (32:7), and by sharing his intent to destroy them (32:10). Moses pleads with the Lord to reconsider: "Why does your wrath burn hot against your people, whom you have brought out of Egypt with great power and with a mighty hand?" (32:11). After the Lord relented from the punishment he had spoken of, Moses went down the mountain, witnessed how the people had broken the covenant, and broke the tablets of the covenant.

The Mosaic law, and the corresponding creation of a new nation in covenant with the Lord, carries the possibility of individual sin which impacts

9. Routledge, *Old Testament Theology*, 147.

the nation. We witness this in the life and death of Achan, a member of the tribe of Judah who stole forbidden spoils from Jericho (Josh 7). His sin led to Israel's disastrous failure against the men of Ai. Once discovered and accused, Achan confessed his sin and was stoned, along with his family and properties. Robert F. Johnson writes:

> This story stands as vivid evidence of the early Israelite conception of the solidarity of the community. The guilt of one threatened the security of all, and the requisite penalty for such guilt must be inflicted upon Achan's total sphere of family and possessions.[10]

In addition to the notion of collective sin, the Mosaic covenant introduces the indispensable role of the priest. Understanding the results of sin as the severing of the relationship between God and his people, the Mosaic law identifies the priest as the mediator who facilitates the restoration of that relationship. The first mediator identified in Scripture is Moses, who effectively pleads with God to relent from destroying the whole nation, except Moses (Exod 32:11–14). On the day after his descent from Mount Sinai, Moses said to the people, "You have sinned a great sin. And now I will go up to the Lord; perhaps I can make atonement for your sin" (32:30). Moses repeated this mediatorial work on many occasions, each time entering the "tent of meeting" and interceding on behalf of the people to God (33:7).

The first official priest was Aaron, the ancestor of all lawful priests. God commanded Moses to anoint Aaron as priest (Exod 29:7). He also commanded Moses to make vestments which Aaron was to wear in the tent of meeting in the holy place (Exod 28; Lev 8:7–9). Finally, God instructed Aaron on how to fulfill his office as priest (Num 18). One of his responsibilities was to enter the holy of holies and make atonement for the people (Lev 16). Another was to facilitate the sacrifices of individuals who desired to make atonement for individual sin (Lev 1). Interestingly, when making atonement for an individual, the Lord prescribed that the individual seeking atonement kill the animal that would then be sacrificed. In contrast, when making atonement for the collective or national sin, the Lord prescribed that the priest kill the animal. In both cases, the animal sacrifice represents the means by which the person or nation seeks to reestablish their relationship with God.

In summary, when we survey the biblical understanding of sin from Abraham through Moses, we find repeated affirmation that sin must first be understood within the context of a vital, dynamic relationship between

10. Johnson, "Achan," 1:26.

God and his chosen people. Surely, those who have chosen to reject God sin; that is to be expected. The biblical narrative, however, focuses on the history of God's people—a sinning people in constant need of forgiveness and reconciliation. The Bible describes sin for God's people as disobedience to his word or rebellion against his will. From time to time, it describes the motives for such behavior: for Abraham, it was doubt in the promises of God, and for the people of God in the plain of Sinai, it was fear that their leader was dead.

In this period of biblical history, we also discover two important developments with respect to sin. First, by creating a new theocracy, God makes possible a new category of sin: collective or national sin. This is in addition to the earlier understanding of individual sin. Second, within the new theocracy, God created the office of mediator or priest, that person who appears before God on behalf of the nation in order to seek reconciliation between God and his wayward people. In so doing, God reveals the severity of sin. It is not simply a violation of a moral code or the failure to obey a rule. It severs a person's or a people's relationship with the Lord.

THE PROPHETIC TRADITION

The prophets (Heb. *nabi'im*) were the shepherds of Israel *par excellence*. While the monarchy and Levitical priesthood were also sacral offices, the burden for galvanizing the populace to repentance and revival fell on the prophet. For instance, in the absence of a righteous king, Elijah turned Israel back to Yahweh from the precipice of universal worship of Baal (1 Kgs 18:17–40). Though the prophets could occupy a wide gamut of social locations—they could be itinerant preachers, members of prophetic guilds, or court figures and advisers in the orbit of the monarchy—no vocation was as consistent in providing spiritual guidance to Israel and Judah.[11]

Although we often associate prophets with foretelling the future through special revelation (cf. 1 Sam 9:9–24), this constituted a secondary gifting and responsibility. The primary mandate of the prophetic office was to diagnose the people of their spiritual and moral failures and point the

---

11. The Old Testament narratives makes it clear that authentic prophets often endured strained and antagonistic relations to their compatriots, owing to the sharpness of their prophetic message. Waldemar Janzen notes that kings were the most "frequently and directly the target of a prophetic message." Their particular temptation was to revert the nation "back into those ancient Near Eastern modes of thought, life, and worship from which God had redeemed it through the calling of Abraham and the prophetic ministry of Moses." Janzen, *Old Testament Ethics*, 140–41.

way back to covenantal obedience.[12] In short, they were preachers. Interestingly, as House and Mitchell have suggested, as much as 90 percent of the prophetic writings "deals with moral problems we still face today."[13] Micah 2:6–8 provides a succinct example:

> "Do not preach"—thus they preach—"one should not preach of such things; disgrace will not overtake us." Should this be said, O house of Jacob? Has the Lord grown impatient? Are these his deeds? Do not my words do good to him who walks uprightly? But lately my people have risen up as an enemy; you strip the rich robe from those who pass by trusting with no thought of war. (ESV)

Given the size of the prophetic corpus, we will restrict our focus to several prominent forthtelling themes. First, *obedience above sacrifice*. Genuine prophets of the Lord evinced far deeper concern for the motivation and inner disposition of the children of God than with the mechanics of sacrifice and worship, without discounting the latter (see Matt 23:23 for Jesus' prophetic appraisal of the Pharisees). Samuel's diatribe against the faulty leadership of an impatient King Saul—in which said king is also essentially dispossessed of his throne—constitutes one of the cardinal texts:

> Has the Lord as great delight in burnt offerings and sacrifices, as in obeying the voice of the Lord? Behold, to obey is better than sacrifice, and to listen than the fat of rams. For rebellion is as the sin of divination, and presumption is as iniquity and idolatry. Because you rejected the word of the Lord, He has also rejected you from being king. (1 Sam 15:22–23, ESV)

A further regression of the tendency to place correct forms of worship above moral and covenantal obedience can be seen in the willingness of the Israelites to rely on their possession of the proper equipment to deter God's judgment. Consider the words of Jeremiah:

> The word that came to Jeremiah from the Lord: Stand in the gate of the Lord's house, and proclaim there this word, and say, Hear the word of the Lord, all you people of Judah, you that enter these gates to worship the Lord. Thus, says the Lord of hosts, the God of Israel: Amend your ways and your doings, and let me dwell with you in this place. Do not trust in these deceptive words: "This is the temple of the Lord, the temple of the Lord, the temple of the Lord." For if you truly amend your ways and

12. Cf. Maston, *Biblical Ethics*, 35–36.
13. House and Mitchell, *Old Testament Survey*, 174.

your doings, if you truly act justly one with another, if you do not oppress the alien, the orphan, and the widow, or shed innocent blood in this place, and if you do not go after other gods to your own hurt, then I will dwell with you in this place, in the land that I gave of old to your ancestors for ever and ever. (Jer 7:1–7, NRSV)[14]

The prophets consistently witnessed to the reality that neither sacrifices nor the mechanics of worship determined one's state before the Lord. For them, the heart of the matter was ethics or obedience.[15]

Second, *justice and righteousness.* The diatribe of Jeremiah also points us to the primary positive ethical ideal of the prophets—justice and righteousness. It is commonly supposed that prophets were the formal foil to the priestly vocation in this respect. However, their apparent antagonism actually derives from the high expectation among prophets that the priests would more effectively guide the people to covenantal obedience. The prophets saved their fiercest ire for the "intolerable simultaneous practice of cultic activity and social injustice."[16]

The preeminent negative precedent which provoked the prophetic condemnation of social injustice was the seizure of Naboth's vineyard by Ahab and Jezebel (1 Kgs 21:1–16). The conclusion of this episode sees Elijah delivering a chilling oracle to King Ahab:

You shall say to him, "Thus says the Lord: Have you killed, and also taken possession?" You shall say to him, "Thus says the Lord: In the place where dogs licked up the blood of Naboth, dogs will also lick up your blood." (21:19, NRSV)

The unjust seizure of family land, which was first perpetrated only tentatively by even the monarch of Israel—Ahab needed the extra provocation that Jezebel provided—would later become commonplace.[17] Isaiah rails against the avaricious, relentless expansion of personal real estate: "Ah, you who join house to house, who add field to field, until there is room for no one but you, and you are left to live alone in the midst of the land!" (Isa 5:8, NRSV). No prophet sounded this call more vigorously than Amos, in the eighth century BC:

---

14. Cf. Janzen, *Old Testament Ethics*, 162.

15. Maston, *Biblical Ethics*, 49–50.

16. Maston, *Biblical Ethics*, 49–50.

17. For a survey of the historical situation which gave rise to economic and class distinctions in Israel, see Bullock, *Introduction to the Old Testament*, 29–31.

Hear this, you that trample on the needy, and bring to ruin the poor of the land, saying, "When will the new moon be over so that we may sell grain; and the Sabbath, so that we may offer wheat for sale? We will make the ephah small and the shekel great and practice deceit with false balances, buying the poor for silver and the needy for a pair of sandals, and selling the sweepings of the wheat" (Amos 8:4–6, NRSV).

Third, *the Lord alone is God*. The prophets' clarion call to justice and righteousness was not borne out of populist advocacy for the poor, but the spiritual and theological call of a just and righteous God.[18] To perpetrate violence or economic oppression against one's neighbor was to breach the loyalty and obedience required by the Lord of his people.[19] Justice, honesty, and equity were not so much *rights* of the individual as moral *responsibilities* enacted by the God of Israel. Micah's well-known credo captures the coherent relationship between right living and devotion to Yahweh: "He has told you, O man, what is good; and what does the Lord require of you but to do justice, to love kindness, and to walk humbly with your God?" (Mic 6:8, NASB). The practice of such virtues was indeed an extension of one's devotion to the Lord, which was always at the core of Mosaic faith, despite its external trappings. Prophets were always calling their hearers back to the allegiance demanded by the great credo of Israel, the *Shema*: "Hear, O Israel: The Lord is our God, the Lord alone. You shall love the Lord your God with all your heart, and with all your soul, and with all your might" (Deut 6:4–5, NRSV). It was the unglamorous task of the prophets to maintain that allegiance and prevent the apostasy of their countrymen. Sadly, the resistance of the people to repentance and obedience is written on seemingly every page of the Prophets. This spiritual failure manifested itself not only in violence, economic injustice, and dishonesty, as treated above, but also and most blatantly in idolatry. Isaiah's condemnation of idol worship features withering sarcasm:

Those who fashion a graven image are all of them futile, and their precious things are of no profit; even their own witnesses fail to see or know, so that they will be put to shame. Who has fashioned a god or cast an idol to no profit? Behold, all his companions will be put to shame, for the craftsmen themselves are

---

18. Bullock, *Introduction to the Old Testament*, 29–31.

19. This stands in stark contrast to a construal of violence or injustice as a violation of one's sovereign, individual rights. That is, of course, part of the political paradigm which undergirds the ethical life of the modern Western world.

mere men. Let them all assemble themselves, let them stand up, let them tremble, let them together be put to shame.

The man shapes iron into a cutting tool and does his work over the coals, fashioning it with hammers and working it with his strong arm. He also gets hungry and his strength fails; he drinks no water and becomes weary. Another shapes wood, he extends a measuring line; he outlines it with red chalk. He works it with planes and outlines it with a compass, and makes it like the form of a man, like the beauty of man, so that it may sit in a house. Surely he cuts cedars for himself, and takes a cypress or an oak and raises it for himself among the trees of the forest. He plants a fir, and the rain makes it grow. Then it becomes something for a man to burn, so he takes one of them and warms himself; he also makes a fire to bake bread. He also makes a god and worships it; he makes it a graven image and falls down before it. Half of it he burns in the fire; over this half he eats meat as he roasts a roast and is satisfied. He also warms himself and says, "Aha! I am warm, I have seen the fire." But the rest of it he makes into a god, his graven image. He falls down before it and worships; he also prays to it and says, "Deliver me, for you are my god." (Isa 44:9–17, NASB)

Jeremiah is similarly scathing in his denunciation of idolatry (e.g., Jer 4:1; 10:5; 18:15). Yet far more was at stake than simply showing one to be a spiritual simpleton, engaged in a farce borne out of poor judgment. Idolatry was closely associated with the moral horrors of Israel's benighted neighbors, and ultimately with the commission of spiritual adultery against Yahweh:

But you trusted in your beauty, and played the whore because of your fame, and lavished your whorings on any passer-by. You took some of your garments, and made for yourself colorful shrines, and on them played the whore; nothing like this has ever been or ever shall be. You also took your beautiful jewels of my gold and my silver that I had given you, and made for yourself male images, and with them played the whore; and you took your embroidered garments to cover them, and set my oil and my incense before them. Also my bread that I gave you—I fed you with choice flour and oil and honey—you set it before them as a pleasing odor; and so it was, says the Lord God. You took your sons and your daughters, whom you had borne to me, and these you sacrificed to them to be devoured. As if your whorings were not enough! You slaughtered my children and delivered them up as an offering to them. (Ezek 16:15–21, NRSV)

In summary, while the prophet certainly functioned at times as a "seer" (Heb. *Ro'eh*), the primary function of the prophet was to goad the whole populace—from king to cattle herder—to covenant faithfulness and devotion to the Lord. Thus, both the content and motivation for prophetic preaching derived largely from the Old Testament Law.[20] Prophets often took the role of antagonists, but only because they held the priestly office to a higher standard of ethical rectitude and guidance, and the groups criticized resisted being held accountable. In addition to their occasional oracles on the ultimate destiny of Israel and Judah, the prophets focused on ethical-theological issues. Chief among these were the superiority of obedience (i.e., moral rectitude and spiritual loyalty) to sacrifice (i.e., proper rites and rituals); the necessity of justice (i.e., basic economic equity) and righteousness against oppression, violence, and fraud; and the supremacy of the Lord and his ways over the false gods of other nations, whose cults fostered sexual immorality and even child sacrifice. While cultic and purity issues are sometimes addressed in the Prophets, they devote the much greater part of their attention to ethical and spiritual matters still relevant today.

NEW TESTAMENT ETHICS

The Gospels

Biblical ethics attains its highest and most complete exposition in the person and ministry of the Lord Jesus, as recorded in our four Gospels. Of them, Matthew is perhaps the densest with ethical material (*didache*), including the longer version of the Sermon on the Mount (as compared to Luke). Many of the specific ethical-theological imperatives that Jesus declares are in fact derived from the Hebrew Bible (cf. Matt 7:12; Luke 6:31; Lev 19:18). Yet as Messiah, the agent of God's reign on earth, and the only human being to perfectly fulfill the Mosaic law, Jesus is supremely and uniquely qualified to act as the authoritative interpreter of the Torah. Thus, the familiar formula: "You have heard it said . . . I say to you."[21]

The Beatitudes are the proper place to begin our inquiry, since it constitutes Jesus' longest discourse and has been long recognized as a manifesto on the Christian life.[22] Dallas Willard has argued for a concessive reading

20. Maston, *Biblical Ethics*, 35.

21. There is debate as to whether what Jesus' audience "heard" comprised the Law in its scriptural form, or the oral traditions of the Pharisees (*halakha*)—or perhaps some of both. In either case, the words of Jesus are theologically and ethically binding in a way that supersedes all precedents.

22. As with most biblical passages, there is interpretive disagreement here. Some

of the Beatitudes, yet the admonitions of Jesus which follow are almost certainly "counsels of perfection."[23] We begin with Matthew 5:21–22.

> You have heard that is was said to our ancestors, "Do not murder, and whoever murders will be subject to judgment." But I tell you, everyone who is angry with his brother will be subject to judgment. And whoever says to his brother, "Fool!" will be subject to the Sanhedrin. But whoever says, "You moron!" will be subject to hellfire. (HCSB)

This admonition reveals that the moral standard to which Jesus' hearers had been accustomed was the prohibition against physical murder (Deut 5:17). This moral standard fostered a degree of civil order and social harmony but left the interior darkness of the heart untouched. Internally, one could murder a brother with impunity. Jesus negates this loophole. Sin is assessed not only in the enacted deed of murder—of which most of us will never be guilty—but in abusive, demeaning language (e.g., "You moron!") and even in the interior condition of being angry toward another. Few if any of us can claim to be innocent of the latter faults. Thoughts are the inevitable precursor to actions, which is why Jesus deals with them so assiduously in his account of spiritual maturity and wholeness (Matt 5:48).

We discover another counsel of perfection in Matthew 5:27–30.

> You have heard that it was said, "You shall not commit adultery." But I tell you that anyone who looks at a woman lustfully has already committed adultery with her in her heart. If your right eye causes you to stumble, gouge it out and throw it away. It is better for you to lose one part of your body than for your whole body to be thrown into hell. And if your right hand causes you to stumble, cut it off and throw it away. It is better for you to lose one part of your body than for your whole body to go into hell.

That the Lord addresses men as the instigators and women as the object of lust is not a mere vestige of ancient Near Eastern patriarchalism. It reflects

---

have viewed the Beatitudes as a perfectionist, eschatological ethnic, or only in force for the apostles. We think that it applies to all believers, but that it is more a descriptive of the flourishing of the kingdom of God among people rather than a prescription for personal piety.

23. Thus, for instance, "Blessed are the poor in spirit" is not construed to be a pronouncement on the basis of humility (*tapeinosune*), but rather the concession that *even* the impoverished in spirit are blessed by the nearness and availability of the kingdom. On the inversion of the conventional understanding of the Sermon on the Mount, see Willard, *The Divine Conspiracy*, 138–85.

the reality that men are more forcefully and consistently assailed by sexual temptation than are women, though neither gender is immune.[24] Contrary to the questionable (and apocryphal) exegesis of Origen, Jesus did not advocate any form of self-mutilation here, yet his rhetorical exaggeration indicates the persistence and insidiousness of the illness. No man can congratulate himself simply on having foregone physical intimacy with the wife of another; even to appropriate her in the imagination is forbidden territory. As John Cassian remarked in his *Institutes,* quoting St. Basil of Caesarea:

> "I know not a woman and yet I am not a virgin." By this he means that bodily purity consists not so much in foreswearing women but in integrity of heart. For it maintains a perpetual in-corrupt holiness of heart whether from the fear of God or from love of purity.[25]

Clearly and perniciously, protracted and unresisted lust tends to at once debase and sully its subject, as well as dehumanize its object. We shall have more to say about sexual temptation below, but the central premise is this: while mentality and cognition are always important for the victorious Christian life, sexual temptation originates at the level of biology, and we must not fail to engage it at the level of biology.

In the exchange that follows, Jesus condemns divorce (the dissolution of a binding interpersonal covenant), the swearing of oaths (which reflect conceit and can be used to manipulate others), and the seeking of retributive vengeance. It should be noticed that Christ does not merely set a higher ethical bar for his hearers, but instead presents a fundamental reimagining of the spiritual life. He boldly declares as spiritual pitfalls some things which his audience did not even recognize as unrighteous (e.g., divorce, oaths, interior anger). In the final section (Matt 5:38–48), this reimagining reaches its pinnacle of moral obligation. Jesus exhorts his hearers to respond not merely to violence but shame and humiliation in a posture of poise and friendliness. We must give up our "right" to seek retributive justice. Indeed, Jesus declares that there is no spiritual merit to loving your friends and family, as pagans do the same (Matt 5:46–47).

The accusations which the Pharisees and Sadducees would level against Jesus over the course of his ministry provided fruitful contexts for him to communicate the proper shape of the spiritual life. When certain Pharisees and lawyers observed that the rabbi and his disciples were eating with unwashed—and thus defiled—hands, Jesus excoriates them:

24. Of course, men also consistently are perpetrators of sexual harassment and sexual violence (in the aggregate), and nothing noted here is meant to exculpate males.

25. John Cassian, *Institutes* 6.19.

He said to them, "Isaiah prophesied rightly about you hypocrites, as it is written, 'This people honors me with their lips, but their hearts are far from me; in vain do they worship me, teaching human precepts as doctrines.' You abandon the commandment of God and hold to human tradition." Then he said to them, "You have a fine way of rejecting the commandment of God in order to keep your tradition! For Moses said, 'Honor your father and your mother'; and, 'Whoever speaks evil of father or mother must surely die.' But you say that if anyone tells father or mother, 'Whatever support you might have had from me is corban' (that is, an offering to God)— then you no longer permit doing anything for a father or mother, thus making void the word of God through your tradition that you have handed on. And you do many things like this." (Mark 7:6–13, NRSV)

Jesus' reply goes beyond the immediate context of defending his actions. Like the prolific prophet whom he quotes, Jesus assesses his opponents as having deceived themselves and profoundly misconstrued the nature of correct spirituality—what an earlier generation would have called "true religion." Jesus goes on:

When he had left the crowd and entered the house, his disciples asked him about the parable. He said to them, "Then do you also fail to understand? Do you not see that whatever goes into a person from outside cannot defile, since it enters, not the heart but the stomach, and goes out into the sewer?" (Thus, he declared all foods clean.) And he said, "It is what comes out of a person that defiles. For it is from within, from the human heart, that evil intentions come: fornication, theft, murder, adultery, avarice, wickedness, deceit, licentiousness, envy, slander, pride, folly. All these evil things come from within, and they defile a person." (Mark 7:17–23, NRSV)

Although polemically Jesus was refuting the Pharisees' application of the Mosaic dietary laws (as Mark makes clear in his gloss, 7:19b), his statements about defilement makes a much broader theological point. Whereas his opponents held to a predominantly external and ritualistic view of the holy life, Jesus uses the vice list as a rhetorical device[26] to declare emphatically that it is evil intentions—*thoughts*—which make a person unclean. Of course, this is not to suggest that the Pharisees were pure ritualists and materialists with respect to religion, with no conception of the affections or heart religion. Nor is it historically responsible to ascribe to Jesus a

---

26. Mark is the textual intermediary, but the words belong to Jesus.

THIS WORLD WITH DEVILS FILLED   33

spiritualism which denies the need for any embodied action in religion, as some Christian sects have been apt to interpret him (see Luke 5:14; 17:14).[27] Nevertheless, Jesus locates the origin of sin firmly in the interior landscape, and not in the lapsed observance of religious ritual.

Finally, Jesus' most incisive spiritual critique, addressed in turn to the Pharisees, the Twelve, and the believing community, comes in the Olivet Discourse—immediately preceding the Passion narrative. Matthew 23 comprises an extended polemic against the hypocrisy of the scribes and Pharisees, and in the following chapter Jesus addresses his eschatological return. Matthew 25 is a cardinal text in which Jesus extols the need for vigilance (vv. 1–13) and godly stewardship (vv. 14–30) in light of coming judgment. Theologically and exegetically, Matthew 25 has been marshaled as a proof text for the ultimate duality of human destiny (as in Augustine) and for the eternality of the torment experienced by the wicked (see v. 46). For our purposes, it is significant that Jesus sets forth eschatological ethical standards: the conduct by which we can hope to fare better in the crucible of judgment at the return of the Son of Man. Matthew 25:31–46 reads:

> When the Son of Man comes in his glory, and all the angels with him, then he will sit on the throne of his glory. All the nations will be gathered before him, and he will separate people one from another as a shepherd separates the sheep from the goats, and he will put the sheep at his right hand and the goats at the left. Then the king will say to those at his right hand, "Come, you that are blessed by my Father, inherit the kingdom prepared for you from the foundation of the world; for I was hungry and you gave me food, I was thirsty and you gave me something to drink, I was a stranger and you welcomed me, I was naked and you gave me clothing, I was sick and you took care of me, I was in prison and you visited me."
>
> Then the righteous will answer him, "Lord, when was it that we saw you hungry and gave you food, or thirsty and gave you something to drink? And when was it that we saw you a stranger and welcomed you, or naked and gave you clothing? And when was it that we saw you sick or in prison and visited you?" And the king will answer them, "Truly I tell you, just as you did it to one of the least of these who are members of my family, you did it to me."
>
> Then he will say to those at his left hand, "You that are accursed, depart from me into the eternal fire prepared for the devil and his angels; for I was hungry and you gave me no food,

---

27. One also sees such a tendency in von Harnack and Bultmann.

I was thirsty and you gave me nothing to drink, I was a stranger and you did not welcome me, naked and you did not give me clothing, sick and in prison and you did not visit me." Then they also will answer, "Lord, when was it that we saw you hungry or thirsty or a stranger or naked or sick or in prison, and did not take care of you?" Then he will answer them, "Truly I tell you, just as you did not do it to one of the least of these, you did not do it to me." And these will go away into eternal punishment, but the righteous into eternal life.

Jesus links election not with orthodox confession, but with practice—namely, the practice of deeds of mercy and charity. The righteous feed the hungry, satisfy the thirsty, welcome the stranger, clothe the naked, care for the sick, and visit the prisoner. These commands function both negatively and positively: the righteous practice them regularly, and the wicked simply omit them. No extra malice is required to be a "goat"—only neglect of one's neighbor. This brand of mercy and compassion is modeled on Jesus' own person and ministry, and thus constitutes the very nucleus of our spiritual aspiration.

Having surveyed Jesus' central teachings on sin and the pitfalls of the spiritual life, we turn now reflect on the writings of some of Jesus' closest friends and followers: James, John, Peter, and Paul. These four apostles were some of the pillars of the early church and are reliable guides for disciples today.

The Epistle of James

James, an apostle and authoritative teacher about the Christ-life, authored our general or catholic epistle of the same name. Although a witness to much of Jesus' ministry, he did not initially believe in Jesus (John 7:5). We learn from Paul that James' conversion was precipitated by seeing the resurrected Lord (1 Cor 15:7). He would go on to become a leader in the early church at Jerusalem, even serving as spokesperson for the apostolic leadership at the Jerusalem Council (Acts 15).

The letter which bears his name is directed to the Jewish Christians of the Dispersion. While it contains less christological content than the letters of Paul, it has been much beloved for its vividness and straightforward spiritual counsel. Significantly, James gives us a brief but incisive description of the cause of personal sin. In James 1:13–16, he writes:

No one, when tempted, should say, "I am being tempted by God;" for God cannot be tempted by evil and he himself tempts no one. But one is tempted by one's own desire, being lured and enticed by it; then, when that desire has conceived, it gives birth to sin, and that sin, when it is fully grown, gives birth to death. Do not be deceived, my beloved. (NASB)

With those words James makes it clear that sin is not a unitary, singular, and unmediated act, but rather the culmination of a process. The believer is not tempted by God but rather by his own internal desires (Gk. *Epithumiai*). Ungodly desire consented to (i.e., "conceived") results in an actual sin. In a vividly grotesque turn of phrase, James describes the outcome of sin: "sin gives birth to death."[28]

Although James does not develop an old man/new man anthropology, he promotes the need for radical renewal of our persona by identifying sin as the outworking of indulged desires. From his perspective, we cannot tackle the problem of personal sin by simply affirming that we will or will not do some particular act. In some ways, that would be analogous to declaring an ability to deadlift four hundred pounds the first time in a gym. Few have that untrained capacity. Likewise, we cannot simply ask ourselves "What would Jesus do?" dozens of times daily, expecting it to produce new behavior. James makes clear that we must first control, redirect, and reorder our wayward and disordered affections. We must reorient the interior economy of our desires.[29]

James, echoing themes prevalent in the Sermon on the Mount, highlights three threats to the spiritual life: words, pride, and infighting. Words play an essential role in our lives by allowing conversation. More importantly for James, the quality of our spiritual lives never rises above the tenor of our interpersonal speech. He takes seriously the injunction of Proverbs, "When there are many words, sin is unavoidable, but the one who controls his tongue is wise" (Prov 10:19, HCSB). James exhorts his readers to be "quick to hear" and "slow to speak" (1:19). Failure to control the tongue entirely negates one's supposed piety (1:26). In a rapid-fire sequence of metaphors, James compares the tongue to a ship's rudder (3:4–5), a fire (3:6), and a deadly poison or pollutant (3:8). Although the other writing apostles certainly issue commands regarding the speech of believers, none is so adamant that speech reveals and shapes the quality of our moral character and piety.

28. Notably, James' use of "desire" parallels the Pauline and Johannine concept of "flesh" (Gk. *sarx/sarkikos*).

29. To be sure, asking "What would Jesus do?" will produce better results than approaching our moral and interior lives without any structure or vision at all.

In James, pride is typically considered alongside wealth, which he portrays more negatively than perhaps any other New Testament writer (except Luke).[30] While the rich man is proud and seems outwardly secure, he doesn't realize humiliation and destruction await him (1:9–11). Pride lends itself to dishonesty, selfish ambitions, and contentions (3:14–16). It is also present when we presumptuously declare our plans for the future (4:10). For James, the converse of pride—humility and gentleness—authenticate our faithfulness and wisdom, since "God resists the proud, but gives grace to the humble" (Jas 4:6; Prov 3:34).

Infighting is an ecclesial issue to which James returns time and again. Division in the church arises partly from the inappropriate favoritism of rich members over the poor (Jas 2:1–4). James' brief discourse on the nature of true wisdom suggests the actual presence of envy and selfish ambition. He confirms this by inquiring as to the source of the "wars" among the brethren (4:1), and answering, via rhetorical question, that they are once again the unhappy fruit of internal "cravings" (Gk. *Edonon*). Finally, James encourages his readers not to criticize a brother, for in doing so they would become illegitimate judges of the Law (4:11–12).

The Epistles of Peter

The analysis of Christian life in 1 Peter aligns quite neatly with the spiritual paradigm of Evagrius and his *logismoi*. Amid the colorful analogies—which compare Christians to milk-hungry infants and to a living building—the author stresses the need for resistance and non-conformity against the moral onslaught of pagan society. In 1 Peter 2:11–12 we read:

> Dear friends, I urge you, as foreigners and exiles, to abstain from sinful desires, which wage war against your soul. Live such good lives among the pagans that, though they accuse you of doing wrong, they may see your good deeds and glorify God on the day he visits us.

---

30. James very nearly construed wealth as a sin unto itself by conveying it as inherently the cause of economic injustice, oppression, self-indulgence, and even murder; see 5:1–6. However, it is important that we as modern readers do not equivocate wealth with sinfulness. Wealth, as well as poverty, may be attended by spiritual wholeness or dysfunction. In James' day, as in the days of the justice-seeking prophet Amos, wealth was tied to land—a fixed commodity. Wealth was in some ways a zero-sum game; a surge of personal wealth could imply the forcible acquisition of land and thus theft or exploitation of another party. Today, intellectual property constitutes far more wealth than do fixed commodities like land. See Schneider, *The Good of Affluence*.

A recurring motif in 1 Peter is the notion that enduring bodily suffering gives us the moral wherewithal to resist the incursions of sin. Such a person is "done with sin," which in 1 Peter 4 comprises the gross vices of "debauchery, lust, drunkenness, orgies, carousing, and detestable idolatry" (v. 3).

First Peter is more or less bookended by admonitions to mental vigilance that resonate with early desert tradition. In 1 Peter 5:8–9 we read:

> Be sober-minded, be alert. Your adversary the devil is prowling around like a roaring lion, looking for anyone he can devour. Resist him, firm in the faith, knowing that the same kind of sufferings are being experienced by your fellow believers throughout the world.

The call to sober-mindedness, literally to "gird the loins of your mind," recalls the admonition from 1 Peter 1:13.

In 2 Peter, the author early on presents salvation, or the knowledge of God in Christ, as enabling us to "participate in the divine nature" and "escape the corruption that is in the world caused by evil desires" (1:4). This Petrine idea of participation in the divine nature is the foundation for the Eastern Orthodox notion of *theosis* or "divinization." It also leads to a clear description of the essential role of virtue in the Christian life:

> For this very reason, make every effort to add to your faith goodness; and to goodness, knowledge; and to knowledge, self-control; and to self-control, perseverance; and to perseverance, godliness; and to godliness, mutual affection; and to mutual affection, love. For if you possess these qualities in increasing measure, they will keep you from being ineffective and unproductive in your knowledge of our Lord Jesus Christ. (2 Pet 1:5–8)

Later in his second letter, Peter details the catastrophic coming judgment, akin to the destruction of Sodom and Gomorrah and of the world in the day of Noah (2 Pet 3:1–12).[31] The expectation of judgment serves as a goad toward holiness and away from the forms of ungodliness catalogued in the second chapter, including blasphemy and sexual immorality.[32]

---

31. The intertexuality of Jude and 2 Peter suggests to many a late date for the latter.

32. The certainty of judgment also motivated the desert Christians. In one of the *Sayings*, an abba rebukes a brother for laughing when the world awaits judgment. The *Sayings*, or the *Apophthegmata Patrum*, is a collection of the writings of some of the early desert monks and nuns, the most well know of which is Anthony the Great, who moved to the desert in 270–271 and became known as the father and founder of desert monasticism. They are still in print in many versions as the *Sayings of the Desert Fathers*. See Ward, trans., ed., *Desert Fathers*, 17.

The First Epistle of John

Although it is an oversimplification, a theological bifurcation is sometimes drawn between the Pauline focus of Western Christendom and the Johannine focus of the East or Orthodoxy. At any rate, the theological emphases in Johannine writings are important to the monastic traditions of Eastern Orthodoxy. Although 1 John does not have an obviously athletic or ascetical outlook, its focus on the love of God is echoed in patristic writers such as Maximus Confessor. First John does not employ the comprehensive vice and virtue lists found in the writings of Peter and Paul. Rather, the expressions of worldly and personal evil are summed up in a familiar, triadic formula:

> Do not love the world or the things that belong to the world. If anyone loves the world, love for the Father is not in him. For everything that belongs to the world—the lust of the flesh, the lust of the eyes, and the pride in one's lifestyle—is not from the Father but is from the world. And the world with its lust is passing away, but the one who does God's will remains forever. (1 John 2:15–17, HCSB)

Flight to the desert was, for many Christians, the prerequisite to leading a life that transcended those corrupting desires. To be sure, their own predispositions towards sexual lust, greed, and pride came with them, but they forged communities animated by practical, mutual concern (cf. 1 John 3:16; 4:20). Their love of God was reinforced by an authentic confession of the Christ (1 John 4:2–3) and borne out by a commitment to keeping God's commandments (1 John 5:2–3). So understood, command-keeping is not a function of stingy legalism, but of love (John 14:15–21; 2 John 1:6).

The Pauline Corpus

The forensic view of atonement, which draws heavily from the Pauline corpus, dominates conversations about sin and salvation among American Protestants, particularly Evangelicals. Much of the discussion borrows concepts and words from the law court. As Angela Tilby notes,

> Sin is a form of trespass. It involves the breaking of a law. God is the judge, we are guilty. God passes sentence, we are condemned. Christ is innocent of sin yet receives the sentence of death. We are imprisoned by sin, yet Christ was punished for our sins and sets us free. He is still our advocate and pleads for

us in heaven. At the end of our lives we will come before the judgment seat of God.[33]

This forensic view of sin and salvation has been codified by Bill Bright (1921–2003) in his nearly ubiquitous "Four Spiritual Laws," the first of which affirms the love of God the Father for the world, which prompted the gift of Jesus for the salvation of all in the world who believe (John 3:16). Then, drawing exclusively from the Pauline corpus, he asserts that "all have sinned and fall short of the glory of God" (Rom 3:23), that "the wages of sin is death," and that those "who do not know God and do not obey the gospel of our Lord Jesus . . . will be punished with everlasting destruction and shut out from the presence of the Lord . . ." (2 Thess 1:8–9). We are, in short, "enemies of God." This legal predicament can only be resolved through faith in Jesus Christ, who died for us (Rom 5:8), for our sins (1 Cor 15:3).

The forensic view of sin, however, is not the only way the apostle Paul understood sin. Paul understands sin not only as a violation of divine law but also as a principle and power in the individual and in the world. Over a hundred years ago, Orello Cone wrote that, for Paul,

> [Sin] has come into the world, where it has dominion, works concupiscence, slays, comes to life, deceives, does the wrong which the better self rejects, holds men in bondage, and is a force which has a law. The universal sway of this power in human life and history is a capital provision of the apostle's which he undertakes to establish by an injunction from observed facts of sinfulness, by individual experience, and by Scripture.[34]

In addition to more sustained ethical exposition, Paul employs a number of vice lists to describe the character of the God-ignorant and unrighteous (*adikos*)—that is, the lives of his spiritual children before meeting Christ. One such passage is Galatians 5:19–21:

> Now the works of the flesh are obvious: fornication, impurity, licentiousness, idolatry, sorcery, enmities, strife, jealousy, anger, quarrels, dissensions, factions, envy, drunkenness, carousing, and things like these. I am warning you, as I warned you before: those who do such things will not inherit the kingdom of God. (NRSV)

Another such passage is 1 Corinthians 6:9–10:

---

33. Tilby, *Seven Deadly Sins*, 5.

34. Cone, "Pauline Doctrine of Sin," 242.

> You know that wicked people will not inherit the kingdom of God,
> don't you? Stop deceiving yourselves! Sexually immoral people,
> idolaters, adulterers, male prostitutes, homosexuals,[35] thieves,
> greedy people, drunks, slanderers, and robbers will not inherit
> the kingdom of God. (ISV)

One important aspect of these vice lists: Paul does not spend any time creating a hierarchy of sin or stigmatizing one above others. By contrast, Christians today tend to do just that, shunning certain categories of sin and excusing others as innocuous. Paul does not treat such lists as exhaustive, but taken together, they paint the picture of an unregenerate person in Greco-Roman culture.

The Didache

Though not canonical, the *Didache*, or *Teaching of the Twelve*, serves here as a representative document for the character of Christian theology a few generations removed from the apostolic era. A manual of "apostolic" instruction, it likely originated in Egypt or Syria from around 100–150 AD, if it is indeed textually dependent upon Matthew.[36] However, other scholarship indicates its independence from that Gospel, and thus perhaps an earlier date. From the outset, it draws a stark distinction between "the way of life" and "the way of death."

Like the New Testament documents, it uses numerous vice lists, and in this case they are even more extensive. For example, "The Way of Death is . . . wicked and full of cursing, murders, adulteries, lusts, fornications, thefts, idolatries, witchcrafts, charms, robberies, false witness, hypocrisies, a double heart, fraud, pride, malice, stubbornness, covetousness, foul speech, jealousy, impudence, haughtiness, boastfulness."[37] The way of life is summarized as "love the God who made thee, secondly, thy neighbor as thyself; and whatsoever thou wouldst not have done to thyself, do not thou to another."[38] The practices outlined as the way of life are to be imparted to the neophyte as a prerequisite for becoming a candidate for baptism, which according to the *Didache* was considered a foundational act for Christian life.

---

35. Certain exegetical voices have insisted that there is ambiguity in the terms *malakoi* and *arsenokoitai*. Most modern Bible translations opt for terms which denote male homosexual partners.

36. For a more technical discussion of the critical issues in the *Didache*, see Milavec, trans., *Didache*.

37. Milavec, trans., *Didache* 5.

38. Milavec, trans., *Didache* 1.

CONCLUSION

Why this overview of sin in the Scriptures? It seems that modern people have pretty much abandoned the concept of sin, having chosen to embrace, instead, an overly optimistic view of human nature. Consequently, even some good churchgoing folk have replaced "saved a wretch like me" in the classic hymn "Amazing Grace" with "saved and strengthened me." Given the right structures in society, all will be well, so we tend to think. As a result, just about everything that goes wrong in life is someone's or some system's fault—and worthy of litigation.

Christ-followers, in contrast, while acknowledging the reality of systemic evil, also affirm the reality of individual sin. Scripture allows no deviation on this point. Hence, we readily acknowledge human beings are sinners in need of forgiveness. As William Golding prophesied in his classic novel *Lord of the Flies*, left to ourselves, we will inevitably descend into savagery. Which is not to say that we are as bad as we can be, but that "we have some perversity in our nature":

> We want to do one thing, but we end up doing another. We want what we should not want. None of us wants to be hardhearted, but sometimes we are. No one wants to self-deceive, but we rationalize all the time. No one wants to be cruel, but we all blurt things out and regret them later. None one wants to be a bystander, to commit sins of omission, but, in the words of the power Marguerite Wilkinson, we all commit the sin of "unattempted loveliness."[39]

---

39. Brooks, *Road to Character*, 54–55.

Chapter 3

The Logismoi

A New and Ancient Paradigm

SAM HAMSTRA JR. WITH SAMUEL COCAR

Our survey of sin has only scratched the surface of what we might call the moral theology of the Bible. In particular, we have by necessity omitted a wide array of more specific sins and vices. Humankind as a whole, in its broken and psychically vulnerable condition, is subject to the whole gamut of these evils. Like Noah's generation, every inclination of our hearts—the seat of our will, thoughts, and emotions—is toward evil.[1] Though each of us undoubtedly has predilections to certain wrongs and a wholesome in-difference to others—a person who would never think of cheating while computing taxes may be tempted to cheat on his or her spouse—still we are all subject to this "world of evil" (Jas 3:6), both in our bodily members as well as the noosphere.[2]

The mention of vices prompts a short explanation of the nature of vices and how we may distinguish them from virtues. We here draw from the fresh Protestant voice of Rebecca Konyndyk DeYoung. In *Glittering Vices* she writes,

1. Willard and Simpson, *Revolution of Character.*
2. The total realm of human thought. This term is thought to be coined by Teilhard de Chardin and derives from the Greek *nous*, for mind.

A vice (or its counterpart, a virtue), first of all, is a habit or character trait. Unlike something we are born with—such as an outgoing personality or a predisposition to have high cholesterol levels—virtues and vices are acquired moral qualities. We can cultivate habits or break them down over time through our repeated actions, and thus we are ultimately responsible for our character.[3]

Furthermore, virtues are "habits or dispositions of character that help us live well as human beings." The late Romano Guardini described them as "living and beautiful" motives, powers and actions in a person gathered as a whole and shaped by an "ethical dominant," the "moral enlightenment" that comes into the soul from the "eternal goodness of God."[4] Vices, in contrast, are "corruptive and destructive habits" that "undermine both our goodness of character and our living and acting well."[5]

While some tendencies may be innate to specific individuals, both "virtues and vices are gradually internalized and become firm and settled through years of formation."[6] That is to say we acquire both virtues and vices through practice or repetition. As sinful human beings, however, our default is vice, not virtue. Hence, the practice that cultivates one is easy, natural, even unconscious, while the other conscious, toilsome, "always endangered."[7] Once acquired, both become second nature. Consequently, we act out from the particular virtues or vices formed within us. As Aristotle taught, vice is a habit that leads to corruption/sin and virtue is a habit that leads to good or excellence.

Vices take a nearly endless variety of shapes and forms. We have already referred to two of the lists included in the Pauline corpus of the New Testament: Galatians 5:19–21 and 1 Corinthians 6:9–10. Centuries later, in perhaps the most thorough vice list ever penned, Peter of Damascus (d. 750) identified 298 distinct vices, including clapping, oversleeping, and flute-playing![8] How could anyone deal with that scope of spiritual onslaught? In fact, it is entirely impossible. To order our lives in such a way as to avoid 300

---

3. DeYoung, *Glittering Vices*, 13.

4. Guardini, *Learning the Virtues*, 4, 9.

5. DeYoung, *Glittering Vices*, 14.

6. DeYoung, *Glittering* Vices, 14.

7. Guardini, *Learning the Virtues*, 6.

8. This list may be found in the *Philokalia*, a collection of writings mostly centering on practicing the virtues and spiritual living in a monastery. It has become an important resource for laity and clergy alike in personal living. The collection was compiled in the eighteenth century by St. Nikodemos of the Holy Mountain and St. Makarios of Corinth.

distinct possibilities for misbehavior would render us at worst dark, mirth-less legalists, and at best hopeless boors. If we hope to avoid vices and, in the process, experience sanctification as Christ-followers, we desperately need a framework that identifies spiritual maladies in a way that allows us to en-gage our enemy courageously and without any hint of being overwhelmed.

We find just such a rubric in the patristic corpus—that is, the writings of the church fathers, as well as the writings of the desert mothers (*ammas*) and fathers (*abbas*). This framework is the *logismoi*—eight categories of the thoughts or suggestions which function as temptations for monks, as well as ordinary Christians, who are seeking a virtuous life. The eight clusters of temptations have been labeled in a variety of ways, but in this treatment as thoughts about food or gluttony, lust or impurity, avarice or greed, anger, sadness or dejection, acedia or listlessness, vainglory or vanity, and pride. The order is important for, as first noted in the desert tradition, the thoughts "move in a sequence from simple to complex."[9] The first three thoughts, for example, flow from one source: food or sex or things (money). The remain-ing thoughts, as we will describe, flow from multiple sources, including but not limited to the preceding thoughts. Dejection, for example, may flow from avarice. Pride, as another example, requires vainglory.

The eight categories of thoughts are not to be confused with the seven deadly or capital sins. Gregory the Great (c. 540–604) is believed to have been the first one to translate the eight thoughts into seven capital sins, cou-pling vainglory with pride. Mary Margaret Funk highlights the shortcoming of equating thoughts with vices or sins:

> Though this terminology of capital sins finds its way into every catechism, the impact of the thinking, which generates our act-ing, was sometimes ignored. The emphasis on sin, which this change in terminology effected, tended to distort the earlier emphasis on the richness of the interior life of a serious seeker who, by striving toward the purity of heart, longs intensely for a significant relationship with God.[10]

Granted, there is gluttony the temptation and gluttony the sin. There is an-ger the temptation and anger the sin. But we must insist on the distinction, for temptation is not sin.

The eight *logismoi* or thoughts have their roots in the Christian intel-lectual Origen (185–254), who theorized about demons while engaged in the pursuit of Christian virtue. David Brakke writes, "Origen treated de-mons primarily in terms of their resistance to the human being's efforts to

9. Guardini, *Learning the Virtues*, 6.

10. Guardini, *Learning the Virtues*, 21.

love God and do the good."[11] In the process, he "created a rich and multifac-
eted demonology" in which, among much else, he links demons with temptations to sinful behavior. More specifically, "Origin taught that individual
demons specialize in particular vices (demon of gluttony, another of pride,
and so on)."[12] He also developed the association of demons with thoughts,
which come either from ourselves or from demons.

Many of the monks of the fourth century followed Origen by focusing
on their own progress toward virtue. The leader of the group was Evagrius
Ponticus (345–399),[13] who is the first Christian thinker on record to ana-
lyze the psychology of sin.[14] Evagrius was born into a Christian family to
a bishop and his wife in the region of Pontus in Asia Minor. He had the
privilege of a good education and was ordained as a reader by Bishop Basil
of Caesarea before being chosen as a protégé of Gregory of Nazianzus. In
383 AD, Evagrius migrated to Jerusalem, where he became a monk in the
monastery of Rufinus and Melania the Elder. It was Melania who persuaded
Evagrius to take up the monastic life in Upper Egypt, where he lived until
death. In the desert, Evagrius quickly emerged as a mentor for other monks.

In his role as a mentor, Evagrius produced many literary works, including his most popular *Antirrhêtikos* or *Talking Back*, a treatise on the
practical problem of resisting demonic suggestions. In this work, we witness
how Evagrius drew from the well of Origen while developing his theory
of eight primary demons, which he also called thoughts. In *Talking Back*,
Evagrius organizes 498 thoughts or situations into eight books according to
the eight primary demons that he claimed attacked monks. Typically, these
eight demons are translated as "gluttony," "lust," "avarice," "anger," "dejection," "acedia," "vainglory," and "pride." Toward the end of the fifth century,
Gennadius of Marseilles referred to the thoughts of Evagrius as the eight
"principal vices."[15] David Brakke notes that "use of the term *vices* reflects the
inward turn in how Evagrius' teachings were appropriated in the West."[16]

---

11. Brakke, *Demons and the Making of the Monk*, 12.

12. Brakke, *Demons and the Making of the Monk*, 12.

13. For an introduction to Evagrius, see Brakke, *Demons and the Making of the
Monk*, 48–77.

14. Tilby, *Seven Deadly Sins*, 4.

15. Thanks to David Brakke for pointing us to Gennadius of Marseilles. Brakke,
"Introduction," 6, in Evagrius Ponticus, *Talking Back*.

16. Brakke writes, "John Cassian had initiated this trajectory by speaking more
frequently of vices than of demons by situating the monk's conflicts with temptation
more within the interior division between the fallen human being's spirit and flesh than
within Evagrius' cosmic division between human beings and demons." From the Introduction to Evagrius Ponticus, *Talking Back*, 6.

As previously noted, in medieval Catholic theology the eight thoughts were modified into the more familiar seven deadly sins. This epithet reflects the Roman distinction between so-called mortal sins and venial sins. It is significant that, while the latter rubric emphasized committed acts, Evagrius and his patristic kin stressed thoughts. The two categories are not synonymous.

Before proceeding to a discussion of each of the eight categories of thoughts, we must address that which lies behind the thoughts—demons or spirits. In the desert tradition, demons are alive and well. Indeed, the terms "demon," "spirit," and "thought" are almost interchangeable in the writings of certain spiritual masters of the patristic era. Such usage was founded upon biblical precedent. Although evil spirits are mentioned occasionally in the Old Testament (e.g., references to the "lying spirit" in Ahab's false prophets, King Saul's afflicting spirit), we see a massive surge in demonic activity in opposition to the ministry of Jesus. In the pages of the Gospels, we see demons behind a wide gamut of human affliction and brokenness. We see demons acting as agents of infirmity, blindness, deafness, self-harm, and violent hysteria. Thus, the machinations of what is termed the "kingdom of darkness" can be observed to result in physical oppression as well as total impairment of one's consciousness or intellect, as was the case with Legion (Mark 5).

But might we attribute demonic influence elsewhere in the New Testament? Paul writes to the Colossians, "See to it that no one takes you captive by philosophy and empty deceit, according to human tradition, according to the elemental spirits of the world, and not according to Christ" (Col 2:8, ESV). The word *stoicheia* is variously rendered, but most translators take Paul to be referring to oppressive demonic forces (see Eph 2:2). Here, Paul associates demonic influence not with demon possession, as commonly understood in Western Christianity, but with distortions in thought patterns and intellectual convictions. The apostle James makes the point that not everything is wisdom which is so called:

> Who is wise and understanding among you? By his good conduct let him show his works in the meekness of wisdom. But if you have bitter jealousy and selfish ambition in your hearts, do not boast and be false to the truth. This is not the wisdom that comes down from above, but is earthly, unspiritual, demonic. (Jas 3:13–15, ESV)

We see that James is heir to the Old Testament tradition which sees wisdom and righteousness as deeply interwoven (as in Proverbs). But it is interesting that he describes a certain kind of (false) wisdom—that is, a certain pattern of thinking and conduct—as demonically inspired.

The church fathers and desert fathers mostly discussed spiritual life in such terms. That is, while a demon or evil spirit may malevolently control a human will (or appear as a monstrous beast, as in Athanasius' *Life of St. Antony*), more often an evil spirit or thought constitutes a temptation, an ideation of wrong, unrighteous conduct. Thus, we recognize a spectrum, ranging from the mere suggestion of a sin—in which the human will is cajoled in some way—to demonization or the subjugation of the human will (e.g., the case of Legion, whom Jesus rescued). Father Maximos of Mount Athos, for one, described this spectrum by identifying five stages: assault (*logismoi* attack the mind), interaction (dialogue with the thought), consent, defeat, and obsession. Any man who, with the help of a computer and the Internet, has wrestled with addiction will relate to each of those stages.

The church fathers and desert fathers also understood the difficult work of wrestling with thoughts as spiritual warfare. In the modern West, one slice of spiritual life is spiritual warfare, which itself consists of exorcism or what is commonly called deliverance ministry.[17] For the fathers, spiritual warfare broadly characterized the whole of spiritual life, and entailed both rigorous assessment of one's interior landscape as well as resistance toward and combat with all the forces which challenge the virtuous and Godward life. So understood, spiritual warfare is not merely a metaphor to describe the nature of the Christian life; it describes reality. The Christian life is a minefield, a battleground, so "watch where you tread. Step off the path and you could end up dead."[18]

We may bristle at the frankness of such a characterization of the spiritual life, but those words are based on Proverbs 3:6; Matthew 16:24; and 1 Peter 5:8. In part because modern Christians have surrendered their distinctive biblical metanarrative to the regnant paradigms of science and psychology, we have an impoverished and contracted view of the spiritual world. Although the secular world has become fascinated with the occult, most Christians seem to make pronouncements on angels and demons only with deep trepidation—if at all. This is not simply a failure of mainline Protestantism. To be sure, there are denominations and traditions where demons are considered simply the bogeys of a premodern, prerational imagination. But the dearth of demonological/angelological language extends to confessional and Evangelical groups. The spirit world is a virtual taboo in these circles. See no evil, hear no evil. Of course, there are exceptions among Baptists

---

17. See Beilby and Rhodes Eddy, eds., *Understanding Spiritual Warfare*.

18. The lyrics of the song "Minefield" by the Christian band Petra articulate a striking and theologically accurate description of the Christian life, one that is entirely congruent with the experience of the committed Christian solitaries who journeyed to the desert to find God and do battle with the devil.

and Pentecostals, Orthodox and Roman Catholic. But even for these, the intersections of *that* world with ours are rare and exceptional events (like *demonic possession* and the corresponding act of *exorcism*), mostly absent from our civilized Western world.

We may also bristle at the description of the spiritual life as warfare out of fear that it may led to the neglect of the call to love God by loving our neighbor. Worse yet, it may help us forget that our real enemy is our own passions and then lead us to demonizing our neighbors, e.g., "Axis of Evil."[19] Granted, the desert fathers and mothers, who were prone to describing the Christian life as war, sought, above all else, direct personal union with God. Motivated by love for God, their preoccupation was not necessarily how to love neighbors. Such an emphasis would have given way to a different paradigm, like that of dying to self or that of suffering love. But their particular presuppositions should not lead to a sidling of the biblical metaphor of spiritual warfare. Nor should our modern concern with the prevalence of weapons and warfare in a world filled with both. We must keep the vertical dimension of our faith in balance with the horizontal, the world as battlefield with the world as mission field, love for God with love for neighbor, putting on the armor of God with picking up the cross.

Given the ubiquity of spiritual warfare against the demonic, we need ways to discern and strategize in our spiritual lives. Towards that end, we turn now to a review of each of the eight clusters of thoughts which recur over and over in the minds of Christ-followers. We will attempt to distinguish thoughts from temptations, even if but theoretically. We will describe the thoughts as created goods but temptations nevertheless that, when dwelt upon or engaged with, lead to either virtue or vice. They function as temptations because they are presented in ways that bend us towards sin. So understood, we are not culpable for the thought itself, though the presence of the thought may be a sign of spiritual immaturity. Still, it doesn't count as sin to have the thought.

We hope that by describing the *logismoi* in this manner we will distinguish between thoughts and sins, as well as resist any correlating pull towards a dualism that views the created order as bad. We also hope that by so doing we will discover a common language to express our shared religious experience as Christians but, more importantly, affirm with the desert fathers that *thoughts matter* and need to be taken seriously. As Mary Margaret

---

19. This phrase was used by U.S. President George W. Bush in his State of the Union address on January 29, 2002 to describe foreign governments that, during his administration, sponsored terrorism and sought weapons of mass destruction.

Funk testifies, "Only when I sensed the power of my thoughts and was able to renounce them could I hear the ever so small voice of God deep inside."[20]

THE TEMPTATION OF GLUTTONY OR HOARDING

Food is central to our existence as living organisms. We must eat and drink to not only survive but thrive as human beings. We must moderate the intake of both food and drink to maintain the physical health necessary for labor and for love of both God and neighbor. We must modify the amount of food and drink we consume out of love for those without either. We must also reflect on how prayers for "daily bread" shape our lives. Do we hoard more than we need while our neighbors go hungry? Do we work seven days a week, thereby failing to observe a Sabbath, in order to store up food for the proverbial rainy day?

Since eating and drinking are essential to life, they figure prominently in all faiths. As the late Karl Olsson noted, "Sacred meals, food taboos, and dietary laws are common to the vast and melancholy range of human religions: through the mouth bane or blessed is received into the citadel of life."[21] The Christian faith, however, differs from others in that it recognizes no food as unclean. While that position did not come without great debate between Jewish Christians and Gentile Christians, "the Pauline-Gentile faith triumphed" and the other position "shriveled away."[22]

The desert tradition begins its categorical list of thoughts with food: when to eat and when not to eat, what to eat and what not to eat, how much to eat and not to eat. Those thoughts arise frequently throughout the day; some come unsolicited and others are prompted by a variety of external or internal stimuli. The desert tradition begins with thoughts on food, not simply because they are foundational to our nature, but because if we can't handle them virtuously, we do not hold much hope for handling more difficult thoughts. As Gregory the Great once said, "As long as the belly is unrestrained, all virtue comes to naught."[23] This explains, as we discuss later, the essential role of fasting in spiritual formation.

The vice associated by the desert tradition with thoughts on food is gluttony. Funk defines gluttony through the lens of John Cassian as "the pattern of eating indiscriminately with no thought of how this food is feeding

---

20. Funk, *Thoughts Matter*, 14–15.

21. Olsson, *Seven Sins and Seven Virtues*, 46.

22. Olsson, *Seven Sins and Seven Virtues*, 46.

23. *Book of Morals: An Exposition of the Book of Job*, 3.6.58, quoted in *Summa Theologiae*, II-IIae, q. 148, a. 1 and 2.

my spiritual life."[24] DeYoung summarizes it as "feeding your face and starving your heart."[25] Frederick Buechner once wrote, "A glutton is one who raids the icebox for a cure for spiritual malnutrition."[26]

Evagrius affirms those definitions. His sixty-nine thoughts on gluttony include when one "desires to be filled with food and drink and supposes that nothing evil for the soul comes from them."[27] He also includes thoughts that the modern reader may not readily associate with gluttony, such as anxiety over where the next meal will come from (16), reluctance to give from our food and drink (49), the practice of collecting food and clothing (50), and the practice of not working for one's food (63).[28]

Given our overabundance of restaurants and our proneness to overeating, it may be difficult for contemporary Christians to view gluttony as sin. Many Americans, in particular, believe they are overweight and harbor a strong and perennial desire to lose weight, but they do not necessarily see body weight as a moral or spiritual issue. Dramatic examples from history, however, give it that cast. The story is told of a certain Roman patrician who spent the equivalent of millions of dollars annually on exotic and excessive cuisines. When he found he had only $400,000 left, he became so depressed at the thought of enjoying simpler fare that he killed himself. Although this seems sordid, the modern West is hardly healthier in its engagement with food than was ancient Rome. Nor is our pathology confined to the upper echelons of society, but instead encompasses all economic classes.

Fundamentally, gluttony constitutes a disrespect for and misuse of our God-given bodies. Biblically, gluttony is viewed as sinful in both its exercise and its effects. Jesus identifies "glutton" as one of the derisive jabs which the Pharisees directed toward him. Paul condemns overeating in his epistles (see Phil 3:19, "their god is their stomach"). As with overindulgence in drink, overeating can render one disinclined to spiritual activity by inducing torpor. Christian cenobites, for this reason and others, were customarily severe in their diets, with many subsisting at length on mere bread and water. Seraphim of Sarov once said, "One cannot see visions of God on a full stomach."[29] The decision by Esau to sell his birthright to his younger brother Jacob for a

---

24. Funk, *Thoughts Matter*, 30.

25. DeYoung, *Glittering Vices*, 139.

26. We thank DeYoung (*Glittering Vices*, 139) for pointing us to this reference. See Buechner, *Beyond Words*, 130.

27. Evagrius Ponticus, *Talking Back*, 6.

28. Indeed, Evagrius and his disciple John Cassian develop a largely physiological discourse on how fasting (and even moderate water intake) "dries out" the body and enables victory over both gluttony and sexual temptation. See Shaw, *Burden of the Flesh*, 147.

29. Seraphim of Sarov, *Little Russian Philokalia* 1:1.

bowl of stew illustrates his point (Gen 25:29–34). Beyond this, however, lies the broader mandate of self-care. To consistently overeat harms our health in ways that can damage or even terminate our usefulness in Christian service. The words of Robert Murray M'Cheyne with reference to his own overwork are relevant here: "God gave me a message to deliver and a horse to ride. Alas, I have killed the horse and now I cannot deliver the message."[30]

In contrast, the creation narratives describe Adam and Eve, in a state of innocence, enjoying the fruit of the garden of Eden in the presence of God. In addition, the Levitical code includes regulations which connect the habits of eating and drinking with our relationship to God, equate mercy with the sharing of food from the harvest, and establish community celebration with feasting. We are not surprised, then, that, in the first century and beyond, wherever you find fellowship in the faith you find food.

THE TEMPTATION OF LUST OR IMPURITY

In Genesis 1 and 2, we learn that God created us as sexual beings, that God wove the sexual dimension of our personality into the very fabric of our identity, and that sexual intimacy between a man and woman existed in the world before sin (it is good). Furthermore, the Decalogue protects the marriage bed from adultery; the book of Ruth, among others, illustrates that sexual intercourse seals the covenant of marriage; the Song of Solomon describes the romantic and erotic attraction between two lovers; and the apostle Paul acknowledges the presence and power of sexual drive while prescribing exclusive and frequent sexual intercourse for married couples (1 Cor 7:1–7). In summary, the Bible teaches that God designed sexual creatures with sexual drive, created marriage between a man and woman as the proper sphere for sexual intercourse and procreation, intended that intercourse between a man and woman would seal their covenant as husband and wife, and encourages sexual intimacy within marriage as a way to strengthen the marriage relationship. In short, sex is good. "The ability to be sexually aroused and desire sexual pleasure is a natural part of God's design for human beings."[31]

Since the fall of Adam and Eve, however, every person enters the world with a proclivity for sin and a unique brand of brokenness with substantial implications for human sexuality. We are tempted to separate sex from relationship, to view sex as an end in itself, to degrade it to nothing more

---

30. This legendary quote has been repeatedly attributed to the Scottish preacher Robert Murray McCheyne (1813–1843).

31. DeYoung, *Glittering Vices*, 160.

than a physical act. Or, as John Cassian and other desert fathers would conclude, we "struggle against the demon of unchastity."[32] When we give into that temptation, we fall into the vice of lust (which we distinguish from the temptation itself). When we allow the vice to have its way, we practice fornication and adultery.

Thoughts on sex are common for human beings, sometimes even while dreaming. These thoughts come from a variety of sources, including memories of past experiences, a chance encounter with another person, and images of an attractive person. The vice of lust is just as common, affecting most if not all of us to one degree or another, including the church fathers, among whom Augustine is exemplar. In his magnificent *Confessions*, a classic of Christian literature, Augustine explains that he was plagued with concupiscence before and after his conversion. He acknowledged that without the help of God he couldn't muster the strength to tear himself away from his disordered sexual desires.

The biblically appropriate ordering of our thoughts on sex calls for both celibacy and chastity. The desert tradition understood celibacy as one part of a call to deny all and follow Christ. As Funk so aptly writes, they described this call in several ways:

> The early monastic fathers thought that if Christ has entered a person's soul, and that person is one with Christ's Mystical Body, his soul enlivened by the Holy Spirit, his body should be chaste, pure, whole, and one with God. Another motivation for celibacy had to do with the end of time. The Parousia (Second Coming) or the reign of God, the early fathers felt, was immanent and therefore human beings should live in the world like the angels, standing in awe, with a clear consciousness of heaven. This path calls one from deep inside to go to God alone without a partner. God alone satisfies our deepest urges.[33]

While some Christ-followers are called to lives of celibacy, all Christ-followers are called to celibacy outside of marriage, and all are called to be chaste. Unfortunately, chastity is often misunderstood as a rule book guiding behavior when, in fact, it is not mere abstinence; "it is the prerogative of the heart."[34]

> A chaste mind helps me refrain from indulging in desiring another's body for my own sexual needs. Chastity helps me simply

32. John Cassian, in *Philokalia*, 6:77.

33. Funk, *Thoughts Matter*, 41.

34. Funk, *Thoughts Matter*, 43.

be before God, in total surrender. When I love God with my whole heart, soul and body, chastity governs how I love. Chastity has to do with my soul.[35]

Furthermore, as DeYoung notes,

Chastity is a positive project, a project of becoming a person with an outlook that allows one to selflessly appreciate good and attractive things—most especially bodies and the pleasures they afford—by keeping those goods ordered to do good for the whole person and his or her vocation to love.[36]

THE TEMPTATION OF AVARICE OR GREED

The biblical creation narratives illuminate many realities, including our relationship to the world. God is the Creator and, thereby, owner of all things. We are stewards who inhabit, manage, and, hopefully, care for that portion of creation apportioned to us. We do so with the "permission of the Creator," while nurturing an attitude of detachment from creation, constantly reminding ourselves that things are on loan to us.[37] We also do so while living a three-dimensional life of love for God, for family/faith community, and for the world, particularly, those whom God would have us give food and drink. This multidimensional life prompts practices like worship of the Creator of every good and perfect thing, faithful stewardship to the Lord and his people, acts of mercy and justice on behalf of the poor, even careful preparation for our futures.

In a post-bartering society, our minds constantly filter thoughts about money: how we earn money and how much we earn, how we save and spend money, how much money we keep and give away. We remind ourselves (or perhaps the Spirit reminds us) that:

Money is intended to be not a god but a servant. This means that, like a good servant, it does its work unobtrusively. It does not call attention to itself but works faithfully in the background.[38]

If money is a servant, the spirit of generosity may prompt us to use it to love God and neighbor. If money is a servant, we will not hoard it or throw

---

35. Funk, *Thoughts Matter*, 43.
36. DeYoung, *Glittering Vices*, 160.
37. Funk, *Thoughts Matter* 55.
38. Olsson, *Seven Sins and Seven Virtues*, 43.

it away. If money is a servant, we will manage it well but also find great joy in mercy:

> The model is the Samaritan with his strong little burro, his travel kit of oil and wine, and his well-filled wallet. We all love that scene: the unfortunate man safely bedded down and out of danger, the innkeeper with his hand outstretched and waiting, and the grave stranger taking two denarii out of his purse and saying with a resoluteness we admire in strong people, "Take care of him; if it costs more, I'll make it right."[39]

That marvelous story may be retold in our lives if we could avoid the pitfalls of the vice of avarice or greed, defined simply by Aquinas as "an excessive love or desire for money or any possession money can buy."[40] We meet the thought of avarice or greed time and again in the pages of Scripture. As with lust, it represents an ungodly and prohibited coveting of those things not one's own (see Exod 20:17). It is especially prominent in the prophetic tradition with its previously discussed emphasis on obedience over sacrifice, and its repeated calls to justice and righteousness. This tradition includes numerous stories of people, sometimes once-faithful people, spiritually shipwrecked by unchecked greed. This was so with Elisha's servant Gehazi (2 Kgs 5:22–27), as well as the tragically undisciplined Achan (Josh 7). When Ahab illegitimately confiscated Naboth's vineyard, the motive was incredible greed as well as pride. It is well known that in the Gospels the Lord Jesus says much more about the economic issues of debt, return, and generosity than about the "spiritual" subjects of heaven, hell, or even prayer. He warns his disciples sharply against avarice—the evil eye which is able to corrupt the whole body, the mammon-desire which competes with God for our devotion (Matt 6:24).

Modern Protestants may be surprised to learn that the desert fathers and mothers, who willfully left the world behind, struggled with avarice. The *Philokalia*, however, reveals that such was the case. Abba John of Karpathos waged a truceless war against this vice.[41] Abba Neilos the Ascetic, who like most in the desert tradition viewed avarice as the fruit of gluttony, asks,

> Why do we attach such value to material things, seeing that we have been taught to despise them? Why do we cling to money and possessions, and disperse our intellect among a host of useless cares? Our preoccupation with such things diverts us from

39. Olsson, *Seven Sins and Seven Virtues*, 45.

40. We thank DeYoung (*Glittering Vices*, 100) for pointing us to Aquinas, *Disputed Questions on Evil*, 13.1–2.

41. *Philokalia* 1:318.

what is more important and makes us neglect the well-being of the soul, leading us to perdition. For we who profess to be philosophers and pride ourselves on being superior to pleasure are seen to pursue material gain with more zest than anyone else.[42]

Abba Maximus the Confessor, in his *400 Chapters on Love*, links avarice to loving a rich person for what he can get out of him or because of self-indulgence.[43] Abba Peter of Damaskos identifies the root of avarice as self-love, referencing 1 Timothy 6:10.[44]

While the monastic tradition prescribes poverty as the cure for avarice, the teachings of John Cassian may be helpful for all Christ-followers, monastic or not. In book 7 of his *Institutes*, Cassian addresses the spirit of covetousness. He reminds us that this demon lies outside of us. It is a "foreign warfare and one outside our nature." As a result, it can be "more easily guarded against and resisted." Once it gets hold of us, however, it takes great effort on our part to root it out. So, Abba Cassian offers his readers detailed instructions on how the spirit of avarice takes root in our souls, which, because of their relevance, are best given in total if but to illustrate the humanness of monks:

> [Avarice] begins by tempting him in regard to a small sum of money, giving him excellent and almost reasonable excuses why he ought to retain some money for himself. For he complains that what is provided in the monastery is not sufficient and can scarcely be endured by a sound and sturdy body. What is he to do if ill health comes on, and he has no special store of his own to support him in his weakness? He says that the allowance of the monastery is but meager, and that there is the greatest carelessness about the sick: and if he has not something of his own so that he can look after the wants of his body, he will perish miserably.
>
> The dress which is allowed him is insufficient, unless he has provided something with which to procure another. Lastly, he says that he cannot possibly remain for long in the same place and monastery, and that unless he has secured the money for his journey, and the cost of his removal over the sea, he cannot move when he wants to, and, detained by the compulsion of want, will henceforth drag out a wretched and wearisome existence without making the slightest advance: that he cannot without indignity be supported by another's substance, as a pauper and one in want.

42. *Philokalia* 1:208.
43. *Philokalia* 2:67.
44. *Philokalia* 3:80.

And so when he has bamboozled himself with such thoughts as these, he racks his brains to think how he can acquire at least one penny. Then he anxiously searches for some special work which he can do without the Abbot knowing anything about it. And selling it secretly, and so securing the coveted coin, he torments himself worse and worse in thinking how he can double it: puzzled as to where to deposit it, or to whom to intrust (sic) it. Then he is oppressed with a still weightier care as to what to buy with it, or by what transaction he can double it. And when this has turned out as he wished, a still more greedy craving for gold springs up, and is more and more keenly excited, as his store of money grows larger and larger. For with the increase of wealth the mania of covetousness increases.

Then next he has forebodings of a long life, and an enfeebled old age, and infirmities of all sorts, and long drawn out, which will be insupportable in old age, unless a large store of money has been laid by in youth. And so the wretched soul is agitated, and held fast, as it were, in a serpent's coils, while it endeavors to add to that heap which it has unlawfully secured, by still more unlawful care, and itself gives birth to plagues which inflame it more sorely, and being entirely absorbed in the quest of gain, pays attention to nothing but how to get money with which to fly as quickly as possible from the discipline of the monastery, never keeping faith where there is a gleam of hope of money to be got. For this it shrinks not from the crime of lying, perjury, and theft, of breaking a promise, of giving way to injurious bursts of passion.

If the man has dropped away at all from the hope of gain, he has no scruples about transgressing the bounds of humility, and through it all gold and the love of gain become to him his god, as the belly does to others. Wherefore the blessed Apostle, looking out on the deadly poison of this pest, not only says that it is a root of all kinds of evil, but also calls it the worship of idols, saying "And covetousness (which in Greek is called *philarguria*) which is the worship of idols."

You see then to what a downfall this madness step by step leads, so that by the voice of the Apostle it is actually declared to be the worship of idols and false gods, because passing over the image and likeness of God (which one who serves God with devotion ought to preserve undefiled in himself), it chooses to love and care for images stamped on gold instead of God.[45]

45. John Cassian, *Institutes* 7.

Who would have thought such thinking would take place in the desert? And who among us does not find him- or herself in that step-by-step description of how natural thoughts and concerns about the future lead first to avarice and then to all kinds of evil? We understand, then, why Paul teaches that the love of money is a root of all kinds of evil (1 Tim 6:10). Money is so attractive that we will commit may sins acquire it. First among these sins is the illusion of self-sufficiency, which incentivizes us to deny our need for God. As DeYoung and others accurately observe, "the possession of money represents this self-sufficiency and the power to secure it, and is a convenient and much less demanding replacement for God."[46]

THE TEMPTATION OF UNGODLY ANGER

Who among us has not drawn vindication for his or her anger-fueled behavior from Jesus, who, after entering the temple courts, overturned tables and chairs while snapping a whip to drive out those selling animals and exchanging currencies (John 2:14 and Matt 21:12)? Upon closer examination, however, we discover that while the biblical accounts describe Jesus' actions, they do not describe him as angry, though it is hard for us to imagine otherwise. Anger seems appropriate for the Son whose Father in heaven burned with anger against an obstinate people to the point of wanting to destroy them (Exod 32:9–10). And who can forget Jesus' anger with the pharisaic Sabbatarian questioners (Mark 3:1–6)? But then here comes the apostle Paul, who, perhaps out of anger, once murdered Christ-followers, warning us against fits of anger (Gal 5:20) and teaching us to put away anger (Col 3:8), before offering this more nuanced approach: in your anger do not sin and "do not let the sun go down while you are still angry," a practice that would "give the devil a foothold" (Eph 4:26–28).

If we take Paul's teaching at face value, we may acknowledge that anger, in and of itself, is not sin any more than laughter. Of anger Karl Olsson writes,

[It] is part of our nature. To live is to desire. To desire is to be frustrated. And to be frustrated is to feel anger. The person who does not feel anger is not a human being and certainly not a saint.[47]

Aquinas represents one of many in the Christian tradition who affirms that line of thinking. He viewed anger as a natural response to threats to

46. DeYoung, Glittering Vices, 111.
47. Olsson, Seven Sins and Seven Virtues, 28.

our well-being or to the well-being of those we love. In his estimation, the movement of anger is natural, and not in our power, hence it cannot be considered sin; furthermore, even the sinless, fully human Jesus experienced anger.[48] The fourth-century desert father Isaiah the Solitary adds another layer to our understanding by describing anger as a passion of the intellect, one without which we cannot attain purity. In his estimation, Christ-followers need anger to flare up naturally in response to "the tricks of the enemy."[49] Evagrius adds that "anger is a useful medicine for the soul at times of temptation."[50]

The acknowledgement of anger as natural and not inherently bad should not, however, blind us to the potential of anger to fuel both good and bad, righteousness and sin. Anger, like electricity, is best handled carefully or it will destroy us. Frederick Buechner once offered these words on the enticing but deadly force of anger:

> Of the Seven Deadly Sins, anger is possibly the most fun. To lick your wounds, to smack your lips over grievances long past, to roll over your tongue the prospect of bitter confrontations till to come, to savor to the last toothsome morsel both the pain you are given and the pain you are giving back—in many ways it is a feast fit for a king. The chief drawback is that what you are wolfing down is yourself. The skeleton at the feast is you.[51]

Few of us, it seems, qualify as spiritual electricians able to handle anger in such a way that it benefits ourselves and others, but the desert tradition serves as a tutorial towards such expertise. The abbas and ammas offer pointed advice for modern Christ-followers on how to disallow anger to establish a foothold within us. They begin by warning us of the power of anger to disturb reason. In contrast to Aquinas, who believed that anger should be regulated by reason, John Cassian believed that anger leads to irrational behavior by diminishing "the insight which springs from an honest gaze."[52]

> If I am full of anger I am blind; I have lost the capacity to give proper counsel and no longer enjoy the confidence of right thinking and acting. My spiritual capacity is diminished and true light is dimmed within me.

---

48. See, as one example, Aquinas, *Summa Theologiae*, question and answer 158.

49. "On Guarding the Intellect: Twenty-Seven Texts" in *Philokalia* I:23, 28.

50. "Texts on Discriminating in Respect of Passions and Thoughts," in *Philokalia* 1:48.

51. Buechner, *Wishful Thinking*, 2.

52. Funk, *Thoughts Matter*, 68.

Evagrius and others concur. They warn that "anger so disturbs reason that it twists any real concern about sin or injustice into service of the self—protecting our own ego, demanding something from the world we would not reasonably expect from anyone else, feeding our own reputations for righteousness instead of admitting our complicity."[53] As Funk writes,

> If I am angry, my heart shifts from a discerning heart to a fuming heart. I think only of my hurts and how I can get even with the perpetrator. I think only of justifying myself; my ego takes over.[54]

There is no better illustration of the seductive power of ungodly anger than that found in Genesis 4. As discussed earlier, Adam and Eve's sons, Cain and Abel, both present offerings to the Lord. God is pleased with the firstborn of Abel's flocks. He is displeased with Cain's offering of produce (Gen 4:4–5) but offers Cain the opportunity to modify his sacrifice and adjust his attitude. Now Cain is at a crossroads—"sin is crouching at the door" (v. 6); he is face to face with the thought of ungodly anger. He may master the thought of ungodly anger or let it fester in his soul. Cain chooses the latter option, which leads him to develop and implement an irrational plan that, to paraphrase Evagrius, disturbed reason and "twisted any real concern about sin or injustice into service of the self." In short, he murders his brother, marking the first of countless murders fueled by ungodly anger.

The challenge before Christ-followers, then, is to allow love for God and neighbor to shape our anger. When anger is so directed, we may describe it as good, even holy. Good anger addresses sin in our own lives, leading to repentance, reconciliation, and restoration with the Lord. Good anger addresses sin that destroys the lives of others, leading to compassion and mercy. Good anger addresses sin embedded in our world systems, leading to justice; it "fights good causes."[55] Yet, even though good anger leads to many good things, the desert tradition encourages us to nip anger in the bud because we tend to handle most anger inappropriately and then sin. Hence, the teaching of Paul remains our most basic guideline: in your anger, do not sin.

53. DeYoung, *Glittering Vices*, 119.

54. Funk, *Thoughts Matter* 77.

55. DeYoung, *Glittering Vices*, 123.

THE TEMPTATION OF DEJECTION
OR WORLDLY SORROW

Western Christians may be surprised by the inclusion of dejection here in that it is not included in the popular and distinctly Western list of seven deadly sins first developed in the Middle Ages. At that time, Gregory, rather than simply adopt the list of Evagrius, modified it by combining the thought of dejection with the thought of acedia, the latter variously referred to as "despondency," "sloth," and "melancholy." While the desert tradition separates dejection and acedia, the abbas and ammas were clear that one can lead to the other, and then empower the other.

The Greek word *lype* (λύπη), from which we derive the word *sorrow*, or *dejection*, can accompany both physical and mental pain, without any connotation of sin. In his second letter to the Corinthians, the apostle Paul distinguished between two types of *lype*: "Godly sorrow brings repentance that leads to salvation and leaves no regret, but worldly sorrow brings death" (2 Cor 7:10). After his prayers in the garden of Gethsemane on the night he was betrayed, Jesus returned to his disciples and found them sleeping because of *lype* or dejection (Luke 22:45). One wonders if Paul viewed the sorrow of the apostles as godly or worldly.

Evagrius does not appear to explicitly distinguish between worldly and Godly sorrow, although his description of sorrow seems to result largely from thoughts about oneself. Evagrius provides the example of sorrow that accompanies "deprivation of one's desires whether actually present or only hoped for." In *Chapters on Prayer*, Evagrius identifies sorrow as a quality of prayer, "the kind one feels when, amid silent groans, he readily admits his sins."[56] John Cassian describes the paralyzing power of dejection when it settles in our souls:

> When this malicious demon seizes our soul and darkens it completely, he prevents us from praying gladly, from reading Holy Scripture with profit and perseverance, and from being gentle and compassionate towards our brethren. He instills a hatred of every kind of work and even of the monastic profession itself. Undermining all the soul's salutary resolutions, weakening its persistence and constancy, he leaves it senseless and paralyzed, tied and bound by its despairing thoughts.[57]

It may be counterintuitive, but the desert fathers and mothers wrestled long and hard with dejection. More specifically, the desert disciple, perhaps

56. *Chapters on Prayer*, 5.
57. *Philokalia* 1:55–56.

reminiscent of Psalm 51, could often feel a lingering despair at his or her commission of a particular sin, or could feel despondent at the lack of spiritual progress.

In the typology of Cassian, dejection or sorrow is one of the *logismoi* that affects us without the possible consummation of a physical act (e.g., sexual lust) and that arises from within rather than being "excited" from without (as with covetousness). As with the other principal "faults" (to use Cassian's occasional language), dejection feeds off and cooperates with the other *logismoi* while retaining its own particularities. It is a more "rational" spirit, deforming our interiority and self-reflection, in contrast to physiologically driven, concupiscible appetites, such as those for sex and inordinate volumes of food. Insidiously, dejection can be disguised as genuine grief over the commission of a sin. However, authentic contrition can morph into dejection if the disciple is unwilling to receive forgiveness, reconciliation, and grace. At this point, pride and presumption have crept in as well: the sinning brother insists he is beyond restoration and presses this point against the elders and the community, who would have him reintegrated. As we find in the *Philokalia*, "There is a breaking of the heart which is gentle and makes it deeply penitent, and there is a breaking which is violent and harmful, shattering it completely."[58]

The desert tradition's dealing with sorrow offers some of the warmest and most human of all the sayings, since they often display the compassionate and pastoral qualities of abbas and ammas known mainly for lives of stern and spartan asceticism. Consider this little pearl from Abba Poemen, aptly known as *The Shepherd*:

> Someone questions Father Poemen, saying, "I have committed a great sin, and I want to do penance for three years."
> The old man said to him, "That is a lot."
> The person said, "For one year?"
> The old man said again, "That is a lot."
> Those who were present said, "For forty days?"
> He said again, "That is a lot."
> He added, "I myself say that if a man repents with his whole heart and does not intend to commit the sin any more, God will accept him after only three days."[59]

Since the experienced desert elders knew how profoundly this demon could harm a disciple, that kind of pastoral care appears with some frequency. Although less visible than some of other thoughts, dejection is no

58. St. Mark the Ascetic, *On the Spiritual Law*, Philokalia 18.

59. Ward, trans., ed., *Desert Fathers*, 99.

less dangerous, for it cuts us off from human compassion and the grace of God, both of which may lead to abject hopelessness. Against this demon, Evagrius prays, "Do not forsake me, Lord; my God, do not depart from me. Come near to help me, Lord of my salvation (Ps. 37:22–23)."[60] What is really going on here? Evagrius describes the passion of dejection this way:

> [Dejection] tends to come up at times because of the depriva-
> tion of one's desires. On other occasions it accompanies anger.
> When it arises from the deprivation of desires it takes place in
> the following manner. Certain thoughts first drive the soul to
> the memory of home and parents, or else to that of one's for-
> mer life. Now when these thoughts find that the soul offers no
> resistance but rather follows after them and pours itself out in
> pleasures that are still only mental in nature, they then seize her
> [the soul] and drench her in sadness, with the result that these
> ideas she was just indulging no longer remain. In fact, they can-
> not be had in reality, either, because of her present way of life.
> So the miserable soul is now shriveled up in her humiliation to
> the degree that she poured herself out upon these thoughts of
> hers.[61]

This passage says two things. On the one hand, dejection has to do with loss. It endures the kinds of loss that constitute normal sadness and grief. On the other hand, dejection also has to do with unreality. It distorts normal sadness and grief into hope for things that can never be.

Saint John Cassian mentions yet another aspect of dejection in his writings. He says:

> Occasionally we are even provoked to fall into this misfortune
> for no apparent reason, when we are suddenly weighed down
> with great sorrow at the instigation of the clever foe, so that we
> are unable to welcome with our usual courtesy the arrival even of
> these who are dear to us and our kinfolk, and we consider what-
> ever they say in innocuous conversation to be inappropriate and
> unnecessary and do not give them a gracious response, since
> the recesses of our heart are filled with the gall of bitterness.[62]

Here Cassian emphasizes the tendency of dejected people to turn away from other people and to turn inward. Both Evagrius and John Cassian illustrate dejection as a disorder of the appetitive aspect of the soul. Our desire is misdirected. Our ability to love life is lost.

60. Evagrius Ponticus, *Talking Back* 4.40.

61. Evagrius Ponticus, *Praktikos* 10.

62. John Cassian, *Institutes* 9.

Clearly, the ancient fathers and mothers of the church were well acquainted with what contemporary psychiatry and psychology call depression. Yet modern Christians suffering with such best understand the ancients within their premodern context. They did not know what we now know about the physiology of brain chemistry. They did not have access to what we have access to, such as the neuroscience techniques of brain mapping. They did not have experience with medically diagnosable and treatable depression as we do. Hence, what they diagnosed as the sin of dejection or godly sorrow we might appropriately diagnose as the medical condition of depression. Consequently, we best be careful not to equate depression with sin. Sadly, in this day and age, too many err in that regard. Still, the subject warrants further exploration. While for the ancients the diagnosis of dejection may have hidden the medical condition of depression, currently the opposite seems to be the case. Speaking from personal experience, the spiritual condition of godly sorrow is often mistaken for the medical condition of depression. One wonders how many therapists are even trained to discern the difference. Here, then, the ancient fathers and mothers provide a valuable resource in helping modern Christians discern the difference between the two.

THE TEMPTATION OF ACEDIA OR SLOTH

Those who respond to the call of Christ by denying themselves and picking up their cross to follow Christ will experience seasons of sacrificial devotion during which they soar on wings like eagles, run without growing weary, and walk without fainting (Isa 40:31). They will have faith to move mountains, hope for miracles, and love for the unlovable. They will love others as they have been loved by the Lord. They will experience harmony among the various practices and parts of their lives. Joy and peace will flow from their hearts.

But those same Christians will live through seasons during which thoughts about the call to discipleship swirl around in their minds. They will question their decision to follow Christ. They will wonder if they should keep running the race and fighting the good fight. They will compare their current circumstances to what could have been. They will imagine the relationships left behind and consider giving up on the relationships they have. In such seasons, as Evagrius observed, days seem fifty hours long. In such seasons, the Christian goes face to face with the "noonday demon" (acedia). In such seasons, writes Gregory of Sinai:

The prince of this world (cf. John 12:31), who campaigns against the soul's incensive power, attacks those striving to attain practical virtue. With the help of the giant of sloth, he continually ranges his forces against us and engages us in a spiritual contest with every trick of passion he can devise. As though in the theater or stadium of some other world, he wrestles with all who stand up against him with courage and endurance; sometimes he wins, sometimes he is defeated, and so he either disgraces us or gains us crowns of glory in the sight of the angels.[63]

Acedia, literally translated "lack of care," is classically translated as "sloth," but may more accurately be rendered "despondency" or "listlessness," even a lack of loyalty.[64] It has been interpreted as a spirit of restlessness or boredom or laziness. With respect to the Christian life, it is, first and foremost, that spirit which hinders the faithful expression of love for God and neighbor—"that powerful sense of responsibility, dedication to hard work, and conscientious completion of one's duty"; it leads to "comfortable indifference to duty and neglect of other human beings' needs."[65]

Evagrius was one of many desert Christians who viewed acedia as the most noteworthy of the eight vices because he believed it tempts monks to abandon their religious lives of love. For the monk, sloth produced a dislike of the place and a disgust with the cell. The disdain then spread to a contempt for the brothers with him. Of the slothful monk Evagrius wrote:

If he doesn't leave the monastery, he stays but merely exists. He has no energy. He is chronically fatigued, He feels hungry, weak, worn out, and tired as if he had just finished an arduous journey. Or he feels as though he has done very very heavy work, or has just finished a two to three day fast.[66]

Siegfried Wenzel adds that "acedia causes the monk to either give in to physical sleep, which proves unrefreshing or actually dangerous because it opens the door to many other temptations, or to leave his cell and eventually the religious life altogether."[67]

Seen in this context, acedia appears rather remote from our contemporary world. We have no cells or religious superiors (most of us, anyway), and so we don't have the opportunity to abandon them. We can mark this line "N/A." But not so fast. As Peter Kreeft perceived, "Nothing so clearly

---

63. Gregory of Sinai, *Philokalia* 4:242–43.

64. On loyalty, and the lack thereof, see Guardini, *Learning the Virtues*, 69–76.

65. DeYoung, *Glittering Vices*, 81.

66. Funk, *Thoughts Matter*, 96.

67. Wenzel, *Sin of Sloth*, 5.

distinguishes modern Western society from all previous societies as its sloth."[68] While we may not have eremitical communities or abbas and ammas, we find ourselves in somewhat similar situations. We have responded to the call of Christ and, as a result, we enjoy seasons of dedication to Jesus Christ and endure seasons of discouragement about our decision to follow Jesus Christ. In the latter, we know what faithfulness requires of us but we can't bring ourselves to care. We take the pedal off the metal, we forsake our daily practices, we neglect our covenantal relationships and obligations, and we go through the motions, bored by each one. Since "busyness and workaholism" are also symptoms of sloth, we may even choose to fill our lives with activity to excuse our sins of omission.[69] All this is the noonday demon at work, robbing "us of our appetite for God, our zest for God, our interest and enjoyment in God."[70]

As people familiar with the history of the people of God, we are not surprised by the prevalence of acedia. We witnessed it in Abraham, the father of our faith. Paraphrasing Gregory of Sinai, who was quoted earlier, Abraham won some and lost some. On some occasions he stood up with courage and endurance; on others he gave up in disgrace. One day he is willing to sacrifice his only son and another day he is willing to give away his wife to a pagan king. But Abraham is not alone in his relational unfaithfulness. Most notably, his experience with the "noonday demon" is shared with the apostle Peter in the early hours of the day when he betrayed the Lord, as well as by most of the apostles, who were not present at noon on the Friday we call "Good." With such notable examples of acedia before us, forgive us if for but one moment we think we are exempt.

We enter dangerous waters when we allow the spirit of sloth to settle in our souls. First, we start refusing the gift of each day; we fail to relish and respond to the graces offered to us daily by God. Then, we neglect the healthy rhythms of work and rest, as well as the repetitive practices that sustain our faith, such as reading and meditating on Scripture, prayer, fasting, service, and our weekly gathering with a local body of believers. In time, like the "prodigal son," we may be tempted to leave the faith for a distant land, one we perceive filled with promise.[71] Or, thinking the proverbial grass greener somewhere else, we may be tempted to leave our church or family or home or city or state. More perniciously, we may even get a seven-, ten-, or twenty-year itch in our marriage, imagining infidelity the solution to our boredom.

---

68. Kreeft, *Back to Virtue*, 153.
69. DeYoung, *Glittering Vices*, 82.
70. DeYoung, *Glittering Vices*, 82.
71. See Norris, *Acedia & Me*, 85.

Faithfulness and loyalty are the virtues that oppose the vice of sloth. The fruit of these virtues for the desert monk was stability—sticking with it. For us it means "remaining true to a responsibility in spite of loss or danger."[72] We realize that God has placed us in a specific place with specific needs, and our job, as Fredrick Buechner put it, is to ask, "At what points do my talents and deep gladness meet the world's deep need?" And then get to it. As David Brooks reminds us, "A person does not choose a vocation. A vocation is a calling."[73] Hence, the abbas and ammas often viewed with suspicion and even contempt the sarabaites or gyrovagues—monks who restlessly wandered, without keeping to a cell, a superior, or a particular order of discipline. It threatened the call to faith and obedience by hardening hearts to the requirements of the Christian life. For the modern Christ-follower, the fruit of faithfulness is, first, the acknowledgment that he or she has been created for and called to relationship with the Lord and, second, "doing day after day whatever it takes to keep the bond of love strong and living and healthy, whether he or she feels particularly inspired about doing it or not."[74]

THE TEMPTATION OF VAINGLORY OR VANITY

One of the first lessons Jesus taught those of us who follow him was to let our light shine before people so that they may see our good deeds and praise our Father in heaven (Matt 5:16), or seek to live in such a way that inspires others to give glory to God and to pursue a more virtuous life. Years later, that teaching was expanded to "whatever you do, work at it with all your heart, as working for the Lord, not for men" (Col 3:23). Centuries later, the Westminster divines declared that our purpose as human begins is to "glorify God and enjoy Him forever."[75] In short, then, we have been called to live out our days before an audience of one from whom we hope to one day hear these words: "Well done, good and faithful servant" (Matt 25:21). Such an approach to life has been described as magnanimous by Aquinas and others, including Rebecca DeYoung, who offers this matchless description:

> Magnanimous people concern themselves with achieving great and hard-won acts of virtue as something to which God has called them. Their achievements are genuinely worthy of honor. They are things that turn our thoughts to the glory of God because they obviously aren't something anyone could have done

72. Guardini, *Learning the Virtues*, 72.

73. Brooks, *Road to Character*, 24.

74. DeYoung, *Glittering Vices*, 86.

75. *Westminster Shorter Catechism*, 1646.

without grace. Magnanimous people radiate God's beauty and goodness in the world, drawing others to that glory, a glory that transcends the person and his or her act. When others witness these acts, their attention is elevated above the one acting and is ushered, momentarily, into the cathedral of God's presence in human action. Acts of magnanimity, whether public or private, large or small, inspire not empty glory but genuine awe.[76]

Do I have a witness? Could this explain why, on March 23, 1743, King George II stood up during the performance of the "Hallelujah Chorus" by George Frederick Handel. Could it be that, for him, the chorus was magnanimous? Could this explain why some Christians seem to perform while others can only be described as "anointed"? When the latter sing or preach or serve, their actions elevate us. Their behaviors point our hearts and minds to the great Artist, the Creator above all creators, and the Giver of every good and perfect gift.

But there is more. We are also human beings, created in the image of our triune God, who long for significance and who fear coming to the end of life only to be viewed as insignificant. Add to that, we long for community within which we can be ourselves and valued as such, within which we are known, acknowledged, and affirmed by others. Here lies one form of our perpetual struggle to live in the world but not be of it, to live meaningfully among people while living before an audience of one.

More often than we care to admit, we lose sight of the one and focus on those around us. We care more about what others think of us than what the Lord thinks of us. When those thoughts are left unchecked, we are overcome by vainglory: an "excessive and disordered desire for recognition and approval from others."[77] We spend our days worried over what others think of us. We say or do things to draw attention to ourselves. We even perceive ourselves through what we think others think of us. The spiritually catastrophic result of such thinking is that we let our light shine before people so that they may see our good deeds and glorify us. Plus, we only allow the light that results in praise to us shine.

Vainglory, "like acedia, which brings to my attention thoughts about what I am thinking and doing, is a secondary thought. It is not about something that I do, but about what I am thinking when I do it."[78] Vainglory speaks to our motivation for behavior, not the behavior itself. John Cassian defined it as doing the right thing for the wrong reason. It is doing something

76. DeYoung, *Glittering Vices*, 65.

77. DeYoung, *Glittering Vices*, 60. See also DeYoung, *Vainglory*.

78. Funk, *Thoughts Matter*, 111.

to gain praise for its own sake. It is behavior motivated by a desire for the praise of those around us, praise which, in retrospect, is vain or "empty, fickle and often off the mark."[79] So understood, vainglory is the opposite of acedia: "reverse sides of the same coin"; by acedia we put ourselves down but by vainglory we place ourselves above.[80]

In the bifurcated cosmology of the abbas and ammas, there is the *world* and the *desert*. Vainglory is not hard to find in the world, especially in the realms of power (such as were graced by polished court scholars, like Evagrius). Here, people show excessive concern for their clothing, bodily appearance, and outward signs of respect in public. But vainglory may also be found in the desert where the vainglorious monk is concerned that other monks be overawed by his long fasts and vigils. His posture is not unlike the Pharisee, of whom the Lord counsels, "Beware of the scribes, who want to go around in long robes and who love greetings in the marketplaces, the front seats in the synagogues, and the places of honor at banquets" (Luke 20:46, HCSB).

For Evagrius, the thought of vainglory took many forms among the desert Christians, including jealousy of others, teaching others before they acquire the health of their own souls, talking about superfluous things, sharing secrets with others, telling others about their way of life, broadcasting through sad appearance their practice of fasting, and boasting in a stable way of life. John Cassian characterizes vainglory as a subtle vice that "insinuates itself by craft and guile into [the] mind," an elusive, inveigling vice, able to exploit both other vices as well as our spiritual achievements:

> If a man fasts openly, he is attacked by the pride of vanity. If he conceals it for the sake of despising the glory of it, he is assailed by the same sin of pride. In order that he may not be defiled by the stains of vainglory he avoids making long prayers in the sight of the brethren; and yet because he offers them secretly and has no one who is conscious of it, he does not escape the pride of vanity.[81]

Vainglory is not hard to find in this world and in today's church. Cleary, it is both opportunistic and polymorphous as we discover countless ways to display our goodness and diminish the glory due to God for it:

79. Sri, "Vainglory: Seeking the Praise of Men."

80. Funk, *Thoughts Matter*, 111–12.

81. John Cassian, *Institutes* 50.11.

The neighbor strives for claim to the greenest, most meticulously groomed lawn. A teenager will only shop at certain stores for name-brand clothes. A business executive wants to drive a certain luxury sedan to maintain credibility and the image of her position. A woman decorates and displays her home for the approval and envy of competitors on Pinterest. Professional basketball players out-dunk each other and decorate themselves with tattoos. A college or company works hard to brand and market itself winsomely. An academic prefers introductions that mention his degrees, book titles, and accolades. Athletes pump their fists and parade around the field with a flag after a spectacular victory. A student carefully decides what to include in various social media profiles and crafts just the right comments on others' posts to elicit the laughter and approval of friends. A pastor is renowned for excellent preaching and feels the pressure to put on an equal 'performance' week after week, even when the well of inspiration runs dry.[82]

Add to that the role of self-promotion on social media, whereby we let our light shine so that others will literally like us by clicking a thumbs up tab. We share all the good stuff we do to increase our audience. We create podcasts and blogs to dazzle people with our wisdom. We do it all without questioning whether such behavior constitutes vainglory.

THE TEMPTATION OF PRIDE

As the patristic period of late antiquity shades into the Middle Ages, so too does the desert tradition. The eight *thoughts* become the seven deadly *sins*; acedia becomes sloth, losing some nuance in the process; vainglory and pride are folded together into the latter. However, since we are interested in the earlier wisdom of the desert, we attend to vainglory and pride separately—even though the desert fathers often represented them together in their spiritual prescriptions—but with an eye to their distinctions. Contemporary Orthodox spirituality affords us surgical precision about the differences. Vainglory initiates pride, and pride completes vainglory; vainglory is concerned with reputation and appearances, whereas pride is concerned about actual agency. The vainglorious person wants others to think he is the greatest; the prideful person[83] wants to *be* the greatest and to destroy those

---

82. DeYoung, "Glorious Things of Me Are Spoken."

83. It is one of the peculiar poverties of language—and thus thought—that the legitimate emotion of taking satisfaction in goodness or excellence is conflated with the vice of self-exaltation: both are "pride." However, being "proud of my daughter"

who would doubt him. Vainglory mutates to pride, as in the broken glory of
the king of Babylon:

> How you are fallen from heaven,
>   O Day Star, son of Dawn!
> How you are cut down to the ground,
>   you who laid the nations low!
> You said in your heart,
>   "I will ascend to heaven;
> I will raise my throne
>   above the stars of God;
> I will sit on the mount of assembly
>   on the heights of Zaphon;
> I will ascend to the tops of the clouds,
>   I will make myself like the Most High."
> But you are brought down to Sheol,
>   to the depths of the Pit. (Isa 14:12–15, NRSV)

Pride, as the consummation of vainglory, is the most pernicious of all
the *logismoi*. It is the first vice to appear in salvation history, but the final test
on the monk's quest for spiritual chastity and union. Cassian calls pride "an
evil beast that is most savage and more dreadful than all the former ones."[84]
Whereas other vices may mar particular virtues (e.g., lust and chastity, gluttony and temperance), pride is singularly destructive of all virtue. Pride is a
"brutal tyrant" who "allows no shadow of freedom . . . to survive in the soul
subject to it."[85] As Mary Margaret Funk observes, "pride is the most deadly
of all the thoughts because it tries to conquer the perfect."[86] Peter Kreeft
calls pride the greatest sin, the one that "comes not from the world, or the
flesh, but from the Devil."[87] C. S. Lewis adds,

> There is one vice of which no [one] in the world is free; which
> every one in the world loathes when he sees it in someone else
> and of which hardly any people except Christians ever imagine
> that they are guilty themselves. . . . There is no fault which makes
> a [person] more unpopular, and no fault which we are more

and "proud of my watercolor painting" are distinct from the spirit of pride discussed
in the fathers. An argument might be made, however, that at least in the latter case an
inordinate love of my accomplishment leads to or constitutes pride.

84. John Cassian, *Institutes* 12.1.

85. John Cassian, *Institutes* 12.3.

86. Funk, *Thoughts Matter*, 124.

87. Kreeft, *Back to Virtue*, 97.

unconscious of in ourselves. And the more we have it ourselves, the more we dislike it in others.[88]

Humility, embodied by Jesus in his incarnation (Phil 2:5-8), opposes pride. As Jesus followed the Father, we are to obey, trusting in the Lord, who "stoops down to look on the heavens and the earth; he raises the poor from the dust and lifts the needy from the ash heap; he seats them with princes, with the princes of their people" (Ps 113:6-8). Modern treatments of humility distinguish the virtue from self-disparagement and self-pity, and prescribe self-esteem as the foundation upon which humility is possible.[89] They remind us that humility is "thinking less about yourself, not thinking less of yourself."[90] The desert Christians, in contrast, exhort one another to humility without feeling the need to define it. Instead, they point one another, and us, to the pre-eminent example of Christ. In his letter to Nicolas the Solitary, for example, Mark the Ascetic writes,

> Keep the humility of the Lord in your heart and never forget it. Call to mind who He is; and what He became for our sakes. . . . Then think to what depth of human humiliation He descended in His ineffable goodness, becoming in all respects like us who were dwelling in darkness and the shadow of death (cf. Isa. 9:2; Matt. 4:16), captives through the transgression of Adam and dominated by the enemy through the activity of the passions. . . . In His great love for man He became like us, so that through every virtue we might become like Him.[91]

But what is the thought or temptation that leads to the vice of pride or the virtue of humility? Is it nothing less than thoughts about our relationship to our Creator? In Genesis 3:1-5 we read,

> Now the serpent was more crafty than any of the wild animals the Lord God had made. He said to the woman, "Did God really say, 'You must not eat from any tree in the garden'?" The woman said to the serpent, "We may eat fruit from the trees in the garden, but God did say, 'You must not eat fruit from the tree that is in the middle of the garden, and you must not touch it, or you will die.'" "You will not certainly die," the serpent said to the woman. "For God knows that when you eat from it your

---

88. Lewis, *Mere Christianity*, 94.

89. Keenan, *Virtues for Ordinary Christians*, 71.

90. Kreeft, *Back to Virtue*, 100.

91. *Philokalia* I:156.

eyes will be opened, and you will be like God, knowing good
and evil."

Here the woman faced the question of her relationship to the Creator—theological anthropology, if you will. From within the framework
of a covenant with the Creator, she responded to the serpent's question by
looking at the fruit and eating it. Unlike the animals, which were "fused
with the reality that surrounded" them, the woman envisioned a future that
transcended her situation.[92] So she broke the covenant and asserted herself
as sovereign. When Jesus faced a similar question from the same serpent,
he responded by quoting Scripture, illustrating the famous dictum of Augustine confessed centuries later: "You have made us for yourself, O Lord,
and our hearts are restless until they find their rest in you."[93] One chose
disobedience, the other obedience. One chose independence, the other de-
pendence. One chose pride, the other humility. In his *Humility Code*, David
Brooks poignantly describes the difference between the vice and the virtue:

> Humility is having an accurate assessment of your own nature
> and your own place in the cosmos . . . Humility reminds you
> that you are not the center of the universe, but you serve a larger
> order. . . . Pride blinds us to our own weaknesses and misleads
> into thinking we are better than we are. . . . Pride deludes us into
> thinking that we are the author of our own lives.[94]

Therefore, echoing Brooks as well as the desert tradition, pride is the central
vice and humility the greatest virtue.

92. Van der Kooi and van den Brink, *Christian Dogmatics*, 255–56.

93. Augustine, *Confessions* 1.1.1

94. Brooks, *Road to Character*, 262–63.

Chapter 4

Excursus

Why Study the Desert Fathers and Mothers?

SAMUEL COCAR

At this point, we undertake a brief excursus to answer an important question, namely, "Why study the desert fathers and mothers?" Two objections typically arise, and we will deal with each in turn. First, "Weren't the fathers just Gnostics who hated the body?" Which is to say, "Weren't they heretics?"

Gnostic, from the Greek *gnosis*, for knowledge, is a broad term applied to a variety of heresies in the early church. These heterodox groups revolved around a common cosmology which exalted the ethereal spirit—the spark of divinity in humans—and denounced physical matter as inferior. Of course, this low opinion of matter extended to the human body (which rendered Gnostics either self-denying ascetics or promiscuous hedonists). Now, the individuals we refer to as desert mothers and fathers affirmed the orthodox and apostolic faith, and so categorically were *not* Gnostics and often refuted them in apologetic works. A few wrinkles, however, complicate this matter.

First, some within the desert tradition strayed from the orthodox Christian faith during their lifetime (such as Tertullian, who became a Montanist), or created highly speculative, extrabiblical cosmologies—often mixed with Neoplatonism—which drew scrutiny and even excommunication (as with the brilliant Origen). Second, and confusingly, the term "gnostic" was occasionally employed with reference not to a heretic but to an advanced Christian disciple, an elder who had begun to plumb the depths of God. Third, the desert tradition harbors an extreme mistrust of the physical body. It was for this reason that celibacy was lionized and associated with spiritual perfection (excessively so among Syriac Christians). Suspicion of the body surely hit its zenith with the luminaries Jerome and Augustine, both of whom viewed the body as a spiritual traitor and a "cauldron of lusts."

While some may find those foibles sufficient to dismiss the entire tradition, we suggest that their mistrust of the body, in particular, makes the desert mothers and fathers invaluable guides to victory in the spiritual life for those who recognize the inseparable relationship between the body and soul. Because of their mistrust, the ancient cenobite, compared frankly to the modern, Western Christian, was vastly better acquainted with the motions of the body: its cues, its idiosyncrasies, its vulnerabilities. Through sustained effort, they developed the science of training the body and mind into Christlikeness. Theirs was a profound knowledge of the physiology and psychology of spiritual life and combat. Even when we might hope for a more life-affirming position, the desert mothers and fathers can mentor us into Christlikeness. We aim to convey at least a sliver of their vast wisdom to the reader.

The male reader may be especially in need of such mentoring. The year 2017 in the U.S. was tainted by revelations of sexual abuse by men in power. Many women broke their silence and told horrific stories of offensive and immoral behavior by men. Many men, your authors included, openly declared that were it not for the grace of God, we too would have been the reason for some fine woman posting "Me too!" Now we look ahead and wonder how we may resist the temptation to use power for selfish gain or to objectify women as sources of pleasure. We realize that no number of rules and regulations will subdue the temptations of power, prestige, and pleasure which arise in the souls of men. Lasting behavioral modification takes place through internal transformation, which takes place through the habit of talking back to the very thoughts that birth sin. No group will serve us better in this regard than the desert fathers.

Second, "What do the desert fathers have to teach me? They didn't have spouses, children, or carpools! Their lives were too different from mine to be of any help." Granted, the social location and daily lives of the desert mothers and fathers differs starkly from our own. They indeed eschewed marriage and sometimes even basic family responsibilities in order to seek out spiritual pilgrimage in the desert (e.g., Antony leaving his sister on her own). Plus, while the church fathers proper sometimes held ecclesiastical offices—the Cappadocians come to mind—most of the desert solitaries were not office holders (although they held church services amid the desert community). You may wonder how modern Christians, embedded in the world, dealing with familial matters, and dedicated to local congregations, gain any wisdom from such a tradition. Don't these differences render their wisdom useless or unintelligible to the modern person?

Perhaps. But might we use the same logic to ignore the teaching of anyone whose faith journey differs significantly from ours? And is that not, in fact, our tendency? We develop our understanding of the faith, one based on our understanding of Scripture filtered through our reason, tradition, and experience, i.e., our personal Wesleyan quadrilateral. Then we allow that understanding to shape our lives. In time we become quite comfortable with our faith and, consequently, uncomfortable with the tradition and experiences of other Christ-followers. Reluctant to be uncomfortable, we create reasons to set aside the traditions and experiences of fellow Christians which cause us discomfort. So, let's write off the desert tradition (and the Pentecostals, as well), highlighting their discontinuity, rather than continuity, with modern Christians. Then we will not have to deal with their call to strenuous sanctification. We can dispose of their extreme example, pleading mortality and overflowing Day-Timers.

But shall we let ourselves off the hook so easily? We think not. First, both the Lord Jesus and the apostle Paul were unmarried, but this does not discourage anyone from appropriating their authoritative spiritual wisdom. Second, countless Christians before us have lifted up the desert tradition as exemplary for their lives. Finally, we need help. Living amid the responsibilities and frustrations of the world does not make it any easier or less important to construct a well-ordered Christian life. We offer this modest handbook to that end. Our intent is not to describe in detail the shape of patristic cosmology or anthropology.[1] The work in your hands is not an academic monograph, but rather a modest handbook on being a more *effective* Christian—one who can leap over the pitfalls common in our spiritual journey. To that end, we conclude this section by reiterating the core insights of the desert fathers relevant to our study.

In the New Thought movement of the late nineteenth and early twentieth centuries, it was frequently asserted that "thoughts are things." The patristic worldview contends that they are often *malevolent* things. The bad ones are considered evil spirits. To have an angry thought or a greedy thought is to be attacked by the demon of anger or the demon of greed. Merely to strive to prevent the associated *actions* is to engage the enemy too

---

1. This term *thoughtworld* was coined by linguist Walter Ong. We use it to signify not merely the explicitly held beliefs of the fathers, but more so the cognitive space in which they operated—the underlying premises which shaped their praxis.

late. As with Jesus and Satan in the desert, the battle begins at the level of query and suggestion: "Wouldn't you like some bread?" Wouldn't you like painless public acclaim? Wouldn't you like an earthly kingdom?"

The anthropology of the fathers and mothers certainly reflected a dualism—that is, a separable mind (or spirit) and physical body. This was part of the Greco-Roman heritage which the church inherited and did not disavow, for the most part. This view is distinct from the more Jewish/OT holism which views the human person as an *enspirited body*. Yet it would be a serious mistake to impute to the fathers the Cartesian dualism which followed them by over a millennium. Desert Christians were not children of the Enlightenment who believed that humans were primarily thinking beings. Rather, they were keenly aware of the effects of the body on the mind and vice versa. For the Protestant reader who finds such a statement theologically suspect, consider the words of no less an Evangelical luminary than Jonathan Edwards: "Such seems to be our nature, and such the laws of the union of soul and body, that there never is in any case whatsoever, any lively and vigorous exercise of the will or inclination of the soul, without some effect upon the body, in some alteration of the motion of its fluids, and especially of the animal spirits."[2] C. S. Lewis asserts a similar perspective through his wily demon, Screwtape:

> Humans are amphibians—half spirit and half animal. (The En-
> emy's determination to produce such a revolting hybrid was one
> of the things that determined Our Father to withdraw his sup-
> port from Him.) As spirits they belong to the eternal world, but
> as animals they inhabit time.[3]

To reiterate the central premise of this chapter: *Spiritual warfare is not the exclusive concern of those needing or performing exorcism. It is a reality for all alive in Christ.* Moreover, the arena in which we have the greatest chance of success—and which Christian solitaries focused on—is that of the mind. Understandably, we have a much better shot at defeating sin if we try to engage it at the point of (demonic) suggestion rather than at the point of praxis. In other words, we ought to engage temptation as such, rather than simply avoid committing sins. In all of this, we are striving to obey the words of the Lord Jesus, who requires of us not merely external compliance, but internal purity as well. In the chapters that follow, we will add more substance to the "new and ancient" paradigm of spiritual life which we have begun to describe.

2. Edwards, *Religious Affections*, 59.

3. Lewis, *Screwtape Letters*, ch. 8.

Chapter 5

The Need for Practice

SAMUEL COCAR WITH SAM HAMSTRA JR.

Before the game, Major League Baseball hitters review the scouting report for their opponent's starting pitcher. They learn that he is hot, having thrown two consecutive complete game shutouts, and that he throws a ninety-seven-mile-per-hour fastball, a curve that falls off the table, a nearly indiscernible change-up, and a quick-cutting slider. They wonder, "How in the world will we hit this guy?"

Having described the *logismoi*, the eight clusters of thoughts that recur over and over and over again in our minds as Christ-followers, we may ask a similar question: "How do we experience victory over these temptations?" That question is a good place to begin. It acknowledges that the *logismoi* represent a formidable opponent. It affirms what the desert abbas and ammas knew for certain: that each day involves struggle with thoughts that form temptations, the options to which are vice or virtue. This "struggle against sin and for virtue is the central drama of life."[1]

But how do we experience victory in that struggle? We suggest that the key to victory on the spiritual battlefield is a disciplined life, a life of

---

1. Brooks, *Road to Character*, 263.

devotion characterized by the regular use of an arsenal of spiritual weapons. Thankfully, we have a large cache of arms and armor for battle. There is no lack of equipment, including, but not limited to, prayer, fasting, Sabbath keeping, meditation, contemplation, solitude, confession of sin, almsgiving, corporate worship, Scripture reading, Scripture memorization, silence, and praying the Psalms. These are some of the more recognizable and transformative spiritual practices for followers of Jesus. There are others, like pilgrimage, presence with the poor, obedience, manual labor, memorial meals, and journaling. Together these practices constitute the spiritual arsenal to which we have been alluding.[2] Some practices are corporate and relational. Most can be practiced by individuals. Each one forms us in some way.

Obviously, identifying such a list is but a modest beginning to the journey of mastering them and ourselves. As handing a woman a sharp sabre does not make her a master in its use, simply having the weapons does not lead to our spiritual transformation. No doubt, in such a case the fencing student would want some understanding of what mastery looks like (a demonstration of the master's prowess would help). Her teacher would require that the pupil spend a considerable amount of time familiarizing herself with the weapon—studying it, carrying it, cleaning it, studying it some more. It would not be strange if the student were required to know something of the history of fencing and the great masters of the pasts (such as Miyamoto Musashi or Domenico Angelo). Lastly, she will practice. She will practice immersively and with keen intent. She will swing the sabre— and thrust and parry—until her arms ache. Perhaps until—as the Scriptures say of Eleazar—her hand cleaves unto the sword (2 Sam 23:10).

We've drawn a martial analogy here, but others would do as well. We cannot merely have the appropriate weapons available to us, although that is a good and necessary start. We must be proficient in them, and for that we must have had considerable prior practice. Jesus is a case in point. His success at facing the adversary in the crucible of the Judean desert was really forged by a profound and intimate knowledge of the law of God—one which could not be conjured up in the moment. We often prefer the painless quick fix, "like a guilt-free diet that demands no sacrifice or the PowerBar that will give us the carbs we need for the next half-hour's activity;" consequently, "we have become consumers of religion rather than cultivators of the spiritual life."[3] But there are no quick fixes in discipleship, and we had better not look for one, lest we find ourselves in a worse state than when we

---

2. See Calhoun, *Spiritual Disciplines Handbook* for an excellent compilation of weapons in our spiritual arsenal.

3. Okholm, *Monk Habits for Everyday People*, 35.

began. Better five smooth stones that fly true from the sling than impregnable arms and armor with which we cannot move.

To make the point again: the ancient Christian masters practiced disciplined lives. They brought to the spiritual battle a received and living tradition about how particular practices of mind and body could repel particular temptations and vices, and how to know they were achieving overall progress in the spiritual life. Sadly, this tradition has been essentially lost to wide swaths of Christianity—not only among modern, Western Evangelicals, but also to ordinary Roman Catholic and Orthodox Christians who are not fully aware of the riches of their respective traditions with respect to spiritual formation, direction, and warfare. Of course, as exponents of the broad Evangelical tradition, as well as pastors therein, we speak most directly to this flock. And though it makes us wince, we begin by addressing the gaps present in the spiritual practices of modern Evangelicalism. These gaps discourage a whole-hearted embrace of a disciplined life and spiritual practices (weapons), which, in turn, leaves us unprepared for battle with the *logismoi*.

THE PLIGHTS OF EVANGELICALISM: FIDEISM, COGNITIVISM, AND GNOSTICISM

It is not new for Evangelical leaders to decry failures in the life of the mind among the faithful. We see this sentiment expressed forcefully from the mouths and pens of thinkers like J. P. Moreland, James Sire, Francis Schaeffer, and C. S. Lewis, who writes:

> The proper motto is not Be good, sweet maid, and let who can be clever, but Be good sweet maid, and don't forget that this involves being as clever as you can. God is no fonder of intellectual slackers than any other slackers.[4]

This injunction applies directly to the fideist, whom Alvin Plantinga describes as one who "urges reliance on faith rather than reason, in matters philosophical and religious," and who "may go on to disparage or denigrate reason."[5]

The habit of placing faith above reason has not afflicted equally all branches of Christianity, or Protestantism in particular. Yet it is troubling how durable is the notion that Christians don't need secular knowledge. The brilliant Jerome, for example, wrestled with the tension of being a Christian or a Ciceronian. In contemporary fundamentalist circles, pursuing

4. Lewis, *Mere Christianity*, 71.
5. Quoted in Amesbury, "Fideism."

knowledge from realms not in direct contact with the Bible may be viewed as dubious or dangerous, a sentiment that may be traceable, in part, to the fundamentalist-modernist controversies of the 1880s through 1920s. In contrast, the lineage of patristic spirituality includes individuals who were both spiritual and intellectual giants, men like Cassian, Evagrius, Origen, Basil, and Gregory. These individuals, and many others like and since them, recognized that all truth is God's truth.

The correlation between spiritual and intellectual acumen—or loving God with heart, soul, mind, and strength—then, is not an accident. Fideism, however it may appear, hinders the life of faith because the fideist cuts him- or herself off from John Calvin's second book of God: the created order. In so doing, the fideist ignores a divine source of truth and becomes gradually disconnected from the faith he or she professes, protects, and promotes. Tragically, we sometimes see Christians reject Augustine or Aquinas or modern theologians because their writings are infected with philosophy. Christians who toss around the term "blind faith" or who set faith at odds with reason accept, to a greater or lesser extent, a fideist vision of the world and a mindless vision of the faith.

Adopting fideism, or a faith that bypasses the intellect, fosters problems that undermine spiritual formation and sanctification. To begin, it is not internally consistent; we cannot fully forsake Athens and embrace Jerusalem. That is, the special revelation of Scripture is communicated in the language, logic, and syntactic structures of human reason. Furthermore, fideism rejects multiple axes of the Wesleyan quadrilateral. The fideist impulse is to ignore reason and tradition, certainly, but most lethal in the context we are considering here is the disavowal of experience. This is because the desert tradition is a body of knowledge—as we have suggested, a somatic wisdom—that pays very close attention to the interactions of body, mind, and spiritual realities. Fideism expressly rejects what cognitivism fails to consider, namely, the sensory feedback of the human body.

Although disciples are expected to make full use of their minds and of reason, another present danger to sturdy spiritual formation is cognitivism. Cognitivists fall into the trap of supposing that the human person is basically reducible to a mind. Cognitivists assume that the best and only path to spiritual formation is the presentation of sound information and well-reasoned arguments. Particularly vulnerable to this trap are Christians in the historic Reformed tradition, with its emphasis on teaching and preaching. Perhaps counterintuitively, fundamentalist traditions may also fall prey to cognitivism, since members often embrace an ahistorical perspective of the Christian faith, a view that dismisses pre-Reformation forms of spiritual formation. What's left for the cognitivist Christ-follower is a weighty emphasis on biblical teaching and an overreliance on sound exposition and preaching to reliably, consistently transform people.[6] This overreliance, then, leads to a neglect of those spiritual disciplines which take place outside the sanctuary and outside the weekly gathering. Solitude and silence, for example, find little time in the life of one busily filling his or her mind with information through books and blogs, podcasts and videos, music and more.

In addition to fideism and cognitivism, Gnosticism poses a third threat to our spiritual transformation. As noted earlier, "Gnosticism" is a broad term applied to a variety of heresies in the early church, each of which exalted the spark of divinity in humans and denounced physical matter as inferior, if not evil. Although it is certainly possible, we assume that you, the reader of this book, are not actively affiliated with Valentinians, Basilideans, or Sethians—examples of the heterodox Christian sects which we conveniently and collectively designate as Gnostic. You probably don't believe in an Old Testament *demiourgos* who is distinct from the divine Father of Jesus, and you are not trying to free your spiritual spark from the prison of your body. Even so, we best be aware that a Gnostic-like virus has infected the church since nearly its beginning and has not yet been eradicated. Such is the case today as it has always been.

Gnosticism reveals itself when we, like those who have come before us, focus not on the sound teaching of the apostles (cf. 2 Tim 2:2) or on the hard work of spiritual transformation, but rather on the secrets or *keys that will unlock* our destiny, purpose, salvation, awakening, or what have you. The end result is a mechanical and incantatory relationship with the Lord. We relate to our Father in heaven not as a divine parent or even person, but as merely a vague, benevolent force or, if personal, the servant of our desires—provided we punch in the right combination of words and rituals.[7]

In the academic circles where we (your authors) live, the label "Gnostic" serves as the ultimate manner in which to delegitimize a person and his or her work. It has much the same effect as labeling someone a "racist." So, we best be careful with the term. We do not want to be alarmists who find Gnosticism behind every nook and cranny, including Evagrius and his kind. But we want to recognize that many of our modern cults are, in fact, Gnostic. Plus, we want to be careful not to approach the classic spiritual disciplines as keys to unlock mysteries or methods by which to pry open

6. Reformed theologian James K. A. Smith offers us some insight into this common, pervasive problem in *Desiring the Kingdom*: "Because the church buys into a cognitivist anthropology, it adopts a stunted pedagogy that is fixated on the mind" (43).

7. For instance, consider the exorcism rite prescribed in Tobit 6:16 in comparison to the straightforward and authoritative exorcisms of Jesus in the Gospels (or the apostles in Acts).

Aladdin's lamp. And we surely want to be vigilant for any tendency to relate to Jesus Christ as anyone other than the eternal, incarnate Son of God.

PRACTICE MAKES PERSONS

Even after rejecting the threat to the disciplined life posed by fideism, cognitivism, and Gnosticism, modern Christians face yet another obstacle to a whole-hearted embrace of the disciplined life. It has been labeled in a variety of ways, but here as "subjectivism," which we define as an overemphasis on feelings to evaluate the quality of our Christian life.

We live in an era in which many Christians unfortunately define the quality of Sunday gatherings and of their own spiritual lives in terms of emotional display and connection. We tend to conclude that if an experience feels good, it is beneficial. Conversely, if a practice fails to generate good feelings, it is useless to our spiritual lives. By describing this tendency as unfortunate, we are not suggesting that dispositions or affections are not fundamentally important to our life in Christ—they are. But we are suggesting that evaluating the quality of our Christian lives on the basis of feelings gives us an unreliable, even false yardstick.[8] When we place this matter before Scripture, we discover it nearly impossible to find crucial spiritual directives which center on feelings—that is, of course, unless we provide a sentimentalist definition of love. Instead, we find countless directives about action and about practice:

- "Pure and undefiled religion before our God and Father is this: to look after orphans and widows in their distress and to keep oneself unstained by the world." (Jas 1:27, NASB)

- "If one of you says to them, 'Go in peace; keep warm and well fed,' but does nothing about their physical needs, what good is it?" (Jas 2:16)

- "Carry one another's burdens, and in this way you will fulfill the law of Christ." (Gal 6:2, NET)

- "But I tell you, love your enemies and pray for those who persecute you, that you may be children of your Father in heaven. He causes his sun to rise on the evil and the good, and sends rain on the righteous and the unrighteous." (Matt 5:44–45)

- "This is how we know what love is: Jesus Christ laid down his life for us. And we ought to lay down our lives for our brothers and sisters. If

8. On the distortion of Christian interiority in modern Evangelicalism, see the excellent: Cary, *Good News for Anxious Christians*, 97–116.

anyone has material possessions and sees a brother or sister in need but has no pity on them, how can the love of God be in that person? Dear children, let us not love with words or speech but with actions and in truth." (1 John 3:16–18)

- "See to it that no one takes you captive through hollow and deceptive philosophy, which depends on human tradition and the elemental spiritual forces of this world (*ta stoicheia*) rather than on Christ." (Col 2:8)

The Scriptures, then, clearly and repeatedly call us to practice our faith—whether we feel like it or not. This practice forms us as Christians because doing shapes our being. In other words, practice makes persons. That dictum, usually attributed to Aristotle, originated with historian Will Durant, commenting on Aristotle's work. Here is the fuller passage:

> Excellence is an art won by training and habituation: we do not act rightly because we have virtue or excellence, but we rather have these because we have acted rightly. These virtues are formed in man by doing the actions; we are what we repeatedly do. Excellence, then, is not an act but a habit.[9]

The ancient fathers and mothers refer to this training or practice as "exercise," "combat," "ascesis," or, as Oliver Clément writes, "an awakening from the sleep-walking of daily life."[10] They believed that the function of practice is to transform, in love, our human nature with the object of making love possible.[11] A prayer by St. Ephraim of Syria gives us an idea of how this transformation works:

> Lord and Master of my life, take far from me the spirit of laziness, discouragement, domination, and idle talk; grant to me, thy servant, a spirit of chastity, humility, patience, love; yea, my Lord and King, grant me to see my sins, and not to judge my neighbor, for thou are blessed for ever and ever.[12]

But what does the principle that *doing* shapes *being* actually mean for our lives? First, clearly spiritual formation goes beyond the direct avoidance of vice—as foundational and crucial as that is. It involves much more than following the dictum "Just say no." Generosity, for example, replaces greed, not by saying "No" to greed, but by the practice of giving generously. We

9. Durant, *Story of Philosophy*, 98.

10. Clément, *Roots of Christian Mysticism*, 130.

11. Clément, *Roots of Christian Mysticism*, 136.

12. Thanks to Clément for pointing us to this "Prayer for the season of Lent in the Byzantine Rite."

cannot even become generous Christians by selling everything we have and moving to the desert, for those who did so constantly wrestled with greed.

Second, we need to practice our faith because subtle non-Christian beliefs and systems creep into our worldview and shape the daily practices of our lives. Consequently, we must constantly—though not anxiously—assess our lives, looking for the values which shape our actions and for the beliefs and assumptions upon which we basis our decisions. An example will make this point clearer.

Let's say you take your kids out to the mall on some Saturday morning. You buy a new video game for your daughter, a baseball mitt for your son, and a new jacket for yourself. You then stop for Mexican food at the food court, refueling yourselves before tackling the second floor of the mall. In the afternoon, you hit more stores, picking up a movie—with the vocal input of your kids—to watch at home and unwind from the day. Running through the day mentally, you give yourself high marks. You didn't yell at little Timmy for running around the store when you asked him repeatedly not to do so. The jacket, which seemed like a bit of a splurge, didn't break your monthly budget. You pushed back that second burrito you felt tempted to devour. You've avoided anger and exercised patience, frugality, temperance, and maybe a little generosity to boot.

But we can probe more deeply. For starters, we must ask, why is the mall a get-to-go place rather than a have-to-go place? Well, obviously, it's *fun*; it's a visually seductive and immersive environment. It is no stretch to call it a temple. While not formally religious, it reinforces the consumerist logic on which it depends with *liturgies*—sights, sounds, rhythms, and the expected, patterned responses of patrons.[13] You reward your children for their good grades with shiny new things. Why? This was a decision, though hardly a conscious one. You could've chosen simply to validate them verbally, hoping this would be more conducive to creating intrinsic motivation or at least low expectations of material reward. You could've chosen an experience—a family picnic or an extra church service. (Ah, but going to church is a have-to thing, not a get-to thing, right?)

You then made the automatic, barely conscious decision to "attack" the second half of the mall, even though you did not need anything more. If you're honest, this was motivated by idle curiosity and the joy of consumption—"Let's see what we find!" You then pick up a movie, patting yourself on the back for finding some PG fare that is not totally mind-numbing, but without any appreciable violent or sexual content. Well done. Notice, though, that you exhausted yourself and your kids on a consumption-centered day.

13. James KA Smith, *Desiring the Kingdom*, 23.

This mental and physical drain is then relieved by two hours of passive entertainment.

If this moral audit seems rigorous, you're right, it is. But not overly so. While we pay a price in convenience, in deserved self-indulgence, in uncomfortable self-examination, we receive a huge reward in return—awareness. We begin to gain an awareness not of the ways in which we have been seduced outright, but of the invisible cultural patterns which have shaped us. And the children of that awareness are freedom, deeper personhood, emotional and spiritual wholeness.

DISCERNING THE SPIRITS

The trip to the mall is but one social script that creeps into our worldview as Christians. There are more. Some are obvious and others not so much, for the many scripts by which society functions, and which are implicitly assumed by neighbors and friends, may be subtle. They are not brazen contradictions of the Apostles' Creed. They are quieter and more insidious, and they force us to look for them. Remember, fish are the last to discover water.

It would be slightly counterproductive, as well as impossible, for us to try and list all of the destructive social scripts and cultural habits we face today. Yet a short list of three may illustrate the challenges we face daily and, then, encourage us to cultivate the gift of discernment—"an ever-increasing capacity to see or discern the works of God in the midst of the human situation so that we can align ourselves with whatever it is that God is doing."[14] In keeping with Paul, and as our Jesuit and Benedictine friends might gently remind us, this is a discernment *of spirits*.

First, excessive introspection or interiority. A great deal of nonsense surrounds dating/courtship and marriage. When do we ever see *love at first sight* in the Bible?[15] But of course, even people who don't believe in this idea start to lose their early feelings of intense, overpowering attraction to their husband or wife. Worried that this is the end of love, they separate or divorce or fret perpetually. Seduced by a social script, these people unfortunately forget that their initial infatuation created a blinding, narcotic cocktail in their brains, and that the covenantal love of Christian marriage is

14. Barton, *Pursuing God's Will Together*, 20.

15. Perhaps only with Jacob and Rachel, and it is doubtful that Jacob had seen many women in his life to that point. Not to say Rachel wasn't beautiful! Kidding aside, this lone instance cannot sustain the weight of biblical normativity, and we must conclude that the idea of love at first sight owes much more to the chivalric tradition and to later European Romanticism.

simple, mundane, companionate.[16] Closely related is the practice of thinking overly deep thoughts about *the need to find themselves*. It is sometimes
just the language that misses the mark; introspection is a great thing in its
bounds, as is differentiation for newly minted adolescents. But this cultural
trope reinforces the idea that there is some self apart from the one that exists
in the world, among other human beings, with responsibilities and privileges (see the double-mind person of Jas 1:8). Far worse when one needs to
find oneself and can only do this by abandoning responsibilities, perhaps to
the partner and children depending on them. It is a solipsistic fantasy and
a demonic lie that we are obligated to search for our authentic selves apart
from the cumber of human ties.

Similar examples of excessive interiority abound and many of them
can shipwreck the process of spiritual formation and excellence. Instead,
as discerning Christ-followers we counter this spirit by choosing to live the
words of the apostle Paul in Romans 12:1–2:

> With eyes wide open to the mercies of God, I beg you, my broth-
> ers and sisters, as an act of intelligent worship, to give him your
> bodies, as a living sacrifice, consecrated to him and acceptable
> by him. Don't let the world around you squeeze you into its
> own mold, but let God remold your minds from within, so that
> you may prove in practice that the plan of God for you is good,
> meets all his demands and moves towards the goal of true ma-
> turity. (JB Phillips NT)

Second, we best beware of reducing the Christian faith to the affirmation of a particular set of doctrines. At least since Constantine, one of the
fundamental deficiencies in Christianity, especially among modern Evangelicals, has been an overfocus on beliefs. So ingrained is our tendency to
delineate Christian from Christian on the basis of doctrinal position that it
is hard to imagine another way. Indeed, it is possible to become so immersed
in the litany of theological options available to us—are we premillennial,
rapturist, cessationist, Calvinist, supralapsarian, open theist, old-earther,
early catholic, sacramentalist—that the very weighty question of what we
have done for our neighbor or in our own spiritual practice becomes uncomfortable, irrelevant, superfluous.

Protestants often trot out polemical tropes about monastics being in-
sulated from the call to love and serve those in the world, but in fact formal

16. David Matzko-McCarthy makes the important point that our culture lionizes
novelty when it comes to sex. Sex cannot be allowed to be merely comfortable or familiar intimacy. *Cosmopolitan* tells us it must forever be *new*. See Matzko-McCarthy, *Sex
and Love in the Home*, 37.

religious orders are often very heavily invested in ministries of benevolence and outreach—as our Roman Catholic readers surely would point out. No, Evangelicals are the ones at greater risk of succumbing to reductionism in this arena; despite all the good counsel we may receive about focusing on the essentials and majoring in the majors, we still identify Christianity basically as a set of beliefs. The active practice of faith, at least in its demanding and unreasonable aspects, usually can be rationalized away comfortably.[17]

It may be jarring, then, to realize that the judgment scenes which appear in the Bible say next to nothing about doctrines or creeds. To be clear, we do not claim that they do not matter. We do claim that biblical judgment scenes are almost exclusively about the divine assessment of our ethical conduct in life. It might not be surprising that this is the case in the Old Testament, where we have little concept of vicarious righteousness and see instead a basic duality between the way of righteousness and the way of the wicked (see Ps 1 and the book of Proverbs). But we also see this in the New Testament. In Matthew 25, the king in Jesus' account of the final judgment announces to the transgressors on his left:

> Depart from me, you who are cursed, into the eternal fire prepared for the devil and his angels. For I was hungry and you gave me nothing to eat, I was thirsty and you gave me nothing to drink, I was a stranger and you did not invite me in, I needed clothes and you did not clothe me, I was sick and in prison and you did not look after me. (vv. 41–43)

To stress the obvious, the king does not grill the "goats" on the Heidelberg Catechism, the Thirty-Nine Articles, or even the Decalogue. It is sufficient to assess the fruit which arose from their belief system—which turned out to be dead on arrival.

Of course, this is just one passage. Consider what the apostle Paul writes to the church in Corinth:

> By the grace God has given me, I laid a foundation as a wise builder, and someone else is building on it. But each one should build with care. For no one can lay any foundation other than the one already laid, which is Jesus Christ. If anyone builds on this foundation using gold, silver, costly stones, wood, hay or straw, their work will be shown for what it is, because the Day will bring it to light. It will be revealed with fire, and the fire will test the quality of each person's work. If what has been built survives, the builder will receive a reward. If it is burned up, the

---

17. David Platt makes this point forcefully in *Radical*.

builder will suffer loss but yet will be saved—even though only
as one escaping through the flames. (1 Cor 3:10–15)

If possible, here is an even more explicit statement about the necessity
of good works. Paul is not necessarily describing a judgment scene distinct
from that of Matthew 25, but he is portraying it from a slightly different an-
gle. In Matthew, there is verbal exchange between the king and the judged.
Here we simply see a fire from God testing the quality of human works.
Although it is a less complete scene, Paul also notes a dual human destiny
in Romans 2. The bifurcation is not about confession, but about virtue and
action:

> But because of your stubbornness and your unrepentant heart,
> you are storing up wrath against yourself for the day of God's
> wrath, when his righteous judgment will be revealed. God "will
> repay each person according to what they have done." To those
> who by persistence in doing good seek glory, honor and immor-
> tality, he will give eternal life. (vv. 5–7)

Consider also the word of the Revelator. Although we must be very
careful in our exegesis of Revelation, the theology and ethics of the book
cannot be dismissed. Reflecting on the final judgment in chapter 20, John
remarks twice that the dead are judged according to what they had done
(vv. 13, 14).[18]

Third, the social script of the "empty self," a term coined by polymath
psychologist Philip Cushman. This is a complex but important subject.
Drawing on the work of Heinz Kohut and several others, Cushman proposes
that post–World War II Western people have been deprived in various ways
of the high-context, meaning-filled environment of traditional cultures.
What does that mean? Imagine, if you can, growing up in a community
without the church and Hallmark calendars, without annual festivals and
rites of passage. Such a context leads to the emptying of the person, for
whom each day is the same as the previous day. No birthdays. No holidays.
No anniversaries. No TGIF. Cushman believed that a person raised in such
a culture will attempt to sooth him- or herself by becoming filled up with
food, transitory experiences, and celebrities.[19] In other words, such a person would be deformed into nothing more than a consumer ever seeking
the next high.

---

18. The penalty for not having done good, and for not being found in the Book of
Life, is to be thrown into the lake of fire—a final and likely painful cessation of human
life (v. 15).

19. Cushman, "Why the Self Is Empty."

It is telling that Cushman, a clinical psychiatrist without overt theological or confessional commitments, incisively diagnosed the spiritual vacuum of modern Western life in many of its facets. In many parts of the world, most notably Western Europe, Canada, and the United States, we find a generation or two of individuals created in the image of God who are not fully human, for the "human being is truly human only in God."[20] Their hearts are restless, for they have not found rest in God. Consequently, they are empty and seek to compensate by filling themselves up with consumables and celebrities. How else do we explain the prevalence of consumerism? Through slick marketing and advertisements, it attacks us relentlessly, promising abundant life if we just drink a beer or dye our hair. And as our wants become needs we succumb with the help of credit cards. Many of our grandparents, in contrast, were immigrants who landed in this country and built a life on that which matters. Shortly after establishing their homes, they pooled their limited resources and built magnificent sanctuaries. After that, they built hospitals and orphanages. But their children and grandchildren, with more disposable income, have managed that which was built but focused on building second homes. We have more than we have ever had but can't give it away, even when our garages are filled with stuff rather than cars. Sadly, instead of giving the stuff away, we have garage sales to make room in our garages for more stuff from the garage sales of others.

The philosophy of the empty self is a force in our culture; it is in the air we breathe. J. P. Moreland helps us recognize it by describing in detail seven characteristics of persons shaped in some measure by the philosophy of the empty self; in his estimation such persons are individualistic, infantile, narcissistic, passive, sensate, void of an interior life, and hurried.[21] The pastoral experience of your authors suggests that four of these characteristics are prominent in today's American Protestant Evangelical church. We have discovered many Christians, ourselves included, occasionally, even permanently stained by individualism, immaturity, narcissism, and passivity. More often than we care to admit, individual Christians have little concern about the needs of the broader community unless meeting those needs helps them achieve their desires, are dominated by infantile desires which must be satisfied immediately, are obsessed by self interest and personal fulfillment, and choose to live through the risks, challenges, and adventures of others. Look at any conflict in your church and you will find these symptoms of the empty self.

---

20. Clément, *Roots of Christian Mysticism*, 263.

21. Moreland, *Love God with All Your Mind*, 88.

CONCLUSION

Living in a world filled with false social scripts, we need to employ the "faith shield" to "extinguish the flaming arrows of the evil one" (Eph 6:16, CEB). The Roman gladiator or messianic warrior that Paul describes in his Letter to the Ephesians with those words makes for a vivid metaphor; it is memorable and makes a great Sunday school lesson for children. But when we probe the theology undergirding it, we ask, what constitutes these flaming arrows? Certainly, they would seem to include that which replaces the filling of the Holy Spirit, including consumerism, sinister thoughts, the defeating or malicious words and actions of others, as well as the ideas of deceptive, anti-God philosophies. It is quite a shield that quenches such attacks!

But what chance does the unarmed person have in the arena? What if the Christ-follower fails to deploy the faith shield? A fascinating and troubling scenario unfolds in the Gospel of Luke:

> "When an impure spirit comes out of a person, it goes through arid places seeking rest and does not find it. Then it says, 'I will return to the house I left.' When it arrives, it finds the house swept clean and put in order. Then it goes and takes seven other spirits more wicked than itself, and they go in and live there. And the final condition of that person is worse than the first." As Jesus was saying these things, a woman in the crowd called out, "Blessed is the mother who gave you birth and nursed you." He replied, "Blessed rather are those who hear the word of God and obey it." (11:24–28)

Jesus here gives a general lesson on the nature of demonization. A person is first successfully relieved of an unclean spirit (v. 24). This spirit, driven out of its "home," seeks rest in waterless places (i.e., deserts) but fails to find anything suitable. It then decides to return to the afflicted person. Instead of finding a person on guard against demonic reentry, the spirit finds a comfortable home—"swept and in good order." It then moves back in with a "legion" of malevolent friends.

This troubling passage seems to suggest that the responsibility for preventing demonic recidivism rests with the afflicted person. After his cure, the demoniac in Jesus' example does not focus on becoming a less hospitable home for unclean spirits. Instead, he remains an empty vessel, fully susceptible to the full-scale demonic invasion on the beachfront of his psyche. Similarly, the empty, consumption-driven person is a clean, well-swept home for unclean spirits. Their focus will always be on the pursuit of personal gratification or on false, unsatisfying social scripts. In short, their passivity will always be a good breeding ground for spiritual vice.

We conclude this chapter with a call to become inhospitable residences for unclean spirits. While this might be in itself a rather large topic, we suggest that part of the answer lies in a life grounded in the disciplined life. Its opposite is a life of dabbling, frivolity, and diversion—in the words of Neil Postman, "amusing ourselves to death."[22] In short, if we hope to experience spiritual victory on the battlefield, we best practice disciplined lives. It is not enough to have faith, as heretical as that sounds. It is not enough to hold orthodox doctrine, though this is important. It is not enough to just say "No." We must practice our faith in order to experience spiritual victory.

22. Postman, *Amusing Ourselves to Death*.

Chapter 6

Foundational Spirituality

The Core Triad

SAMUEL COCAR AND SAM HAMSTRA JR.

More has been written in the area of spiritual disciplines—to say nothing of spirituality at large—than any person could read in a lifetime. This is of course true of theology and biblical studies as well, and yet we feel that new voices should be able to join in the conversation without engaging volumes of prolegomena (a prerequisite for being a German theologian). In this section, we have the modest aim of suggesting the form our daily disciplined life might take.

A good foray into the focus of this section comes from an anecdote from the *Sayings of the Desert Fathers*. Abba Lot came to Abba Joseph and said, "Father, according as I am able, I keep my little rule, and my little fast, my prayer, meditation and contemplative silence; and according as I am able I strive to cleanse my heart of bad thoughts: now what more should I do?" The elder rose up in reply and stretched out his hands to heaven, and his fingers became like lamps of fire. He said, "Why not become all flame?"[1] The reason for the anecdote's popularity seems obvious. It is slightly cryptic and at the same time fascinating. Who among us would not like to see

---

1. Foster, *Prayer*, 6.

patent spiritual manifestations here in our own lives? Abba Lot keeps his "little rule." He prays as he is able, fasts as he is able, and so on. Some might take the story to mean that Lot has a mechanical display of discipline while Joseph has true communion with God, but this seems an unwarranted position, and also imposes a modern, anachronistic dichotomy on the text. After all, we can only control our own actions (and to a somewhat lesser extent, thoughts).

We suggest, therefore, that each Christ-follower can keep the *little rule*. What we cannot control meets us every day. We face financial setbacks, meet and work with difficult people, become ill, and so on. The circumstances we encounter day to day shift and bring with them unique or powerful temptations and spiritual challenges. Likewise, we might have fresh encounters with the fire of God's Spirit, receiving encouragement, deeper insights, and unexpected blessings. These too, while wonderful, are unpredictable vicissitudes. But the *little rule* may serve as the consistent foundation of our spiritual life.

While some may demur that any regularity in one's spiritual life and time with God automatically becomes drudgery and detracts from loving union, we think this is often the battle cry of the undisciplined. While rigidity does not serve us well, consistency does. The disciple who has some form to his or her engagement with spiritual practices will, almost by definition, make more progress than the spontaneous dabbler. This is obvious and becomes even more so when we learn to view Christian spirituality as the path of gaining competence in a comprehensible craft. As Anthony Trollope remarked, "A small daily task, if it be really daily, will beat the labors of a spasmodic Hercules."[2] To return again to our martial analogy, this foundation would consist of the striking, throwing, and grappling skills fundamental to a given martial discipline—say Krav Maga or Brazilian Jiu-Jitsu. We must be well drilled in these if we are to respond decisively to the attack of an assailant (i.e., temptation). The decision to execute a powerful straight punch or a crisp elbow to our nefarious attacker is not relevant, and may even be laughable, if not backed up by months of preparatory practice.[3]

We must then ask which practices form the core of our broader project of spiritual formation. What will be our *little rule*? There will be variations in our answers to this question—this is both predictable and appropriate. The Anabaptist will turn perhaps to the practices of peacemaking and reconciliation, the Anglican looks to Eucharist and spiritual direction, the Calvinist

2. Trollope, *Autobiography*, 80.

3. Luke includes a fascinating vignette of a failed encounter with the enemy in his account of the attempted exorcism by the sons of Sceva (Acts 19:11–20).

looks to conference and edifying sermons. Of course, some of this variation derives from our own varied temperaments.[4] Nevertheless, it will be helpful for us to sketch our own take on foundational spirituality, especially for those whose ecclesial tradition does not give much guidance.

We suggest a *little rule* that includes the three disciplines of Matthew 6: giving, prayer, and fasting. It would be hard to sidestep these practices since the Lord addresses them directly. Furthermore, Jesus introduces each one in a way that assumes their regular role in Christian life:

- "So when you give to the poor, do not sound a trumpet before you, as the hypocrites do in the synagogues and in the streets, so that they may be honored by men." (v. 2)

- "When you pray, you are not to be like the hypocrites; for they love to stand and pray in the synagogues and on the street corners so that they may be seen by men." (v. 5)

- "Whenever you fast, do not put on a gloomy face as the hypocrites *do*, for they neglect their appearance so that they will be noticed by men when they are fasting." (v. 16, NASB)

Clearly the Lord Jesus presumes that his hearers are familiar with and will, in fact, give alms, pray, and fast. He was not, therefore, exhorting them to initiate new practices. Instead, he attempted to recalibrate their posture so that their familiar practices were oriented toward God's glory and not the recognition of others.

The first practice of this core triad is giving. We are quick to dodge the issue of money, so raw is it for us. We can easily rationalize that giving refers to time, talent, and tithe, the latter an option. As such, we minimize the obligation by speaking of the stewardship of time, talent, and treasure. Certainly, God wants and expects those things from us and expects us to contribute to ecclesial life in many ways. However, we should face squarely the issue of material income. It has been noted that Jesus talked about money in its many facets—stewardship, investment, lending, giving, saving—more than the spiritual issues of heaven, hell, and prayer. Surely the disposition of our income reflects our character to an uncomfortable degree (Matt 6:22–24). The Lord Jesus, without question, assumed that giving would form a consistent part of the believer's life. No amount of sophistry and rationalization can get us away from that fact.

We also should not delude ourselves into thinking that money is part of our extraecclesial or non-spiritual life. A number of Christian thinkers in

4. An excellent work on this subject is Thomas, *Sacred Pathways*.

our day have cautioned against the dangers of maintaining a sacred-secular divide in our lives. In this context, such a divide is dangerous because it allows us to think of the spiritual life as a sequestered corner of our person, unrelated to the gritty facts of reality. On the contrary, spiritual formation is about getting us to think and behave aright in our approach to money, sex, and power.[5] Practically, we can understand giving as a disciplined tithe in addition to occasions of spontaneous generosity.[6] A commitment to consistent giving will free us from the worldly anxiety and "evil eye" which run parallel to the money love of which Paul wrote and against which the Lord warns (in Matt 6).[7]

We recognize that some suggest the practice of tithing is not essentially Christian—"We are under grace, not the law." But God sanctioned tithing before the Law of Moses was even given and affirmed the practice after the giving of the Law (Matt 23:23; Heb 7:8). Add to that, the king-priest Melchizedek (who typified Christ) received Abraham's tithes centuries before the Law, and the New Testament does not include a mandate abolishing the tithe. And while we are under grace and not the law, tithing is a spiritual discipline that fosters growth in grace: it functions as an act of faith in God's promise of provision; a tutor for personal, planned, and proportionate giving (1 Cor 16:2); and a weapon for victory over materialism.

Prayer, broadly considered, is communication with God—communication understood "as meaningful, interactive self-disclosure."[8] As Christ-followers, we love the Lord and long to communicate with him. Towards that end, we employ different types of prayer, including confession, intercession, and supplication. But lest our prayers suffer from the gimme syndrome, we include prayers of thanksgiving and adoration. With our prayers of thanks, we highlight the blessings God has poured into our lives. With our prayers of adoration, we honor the giver of every good and perfect gift. Hopefully, our "We thank you for" gives way to countless variations of adoration as illustrated by Psalm 63:

5. Rob Bell is quite right in his assertion that the Bible never uses the phrase "spiritual life." The content of spirituality is that of *life*, lived in communion with and submission to the living Christ.

6. The validity of the 10-percent tithe for New Testament believers is the subject of exaggerated debate. Some argue that since the Mosaic law has been abolished (or, more positively, fulfilled), the giving requirements have dissolved as well. However, the superiority of the New Covenant would obligate us to *more* generous giving, not less! See Acts 20:1–5.

7. 1 Tim 6:10. It should be noted that Gk. *philargyria*, like *pleonexia*, does not refer to the benign desire of improving one's material lot, but rather to a spiritual deformation centered on obsessive acquisition of wealth.

8. Howard, *Introduction to Christian Spirituality*, 300.

> You, God, are my God, earnestly I seek you;
> I thirst for you, my whole being longs for you,
> in a dry and parched land where there is no water.
> I have seen you in the sanctuary and beheld your power and your glory.
> Because your love is better than life, my lips will glorify you.
> I will praise you as long as I live,
> and in your name I will lift up my hands.
> I will be fully satisfied as with the richest of foods;
> with singing lips my mouth will praise you.

Prayer lies at the center of Christian spirituality, whatever strand of Christian tradition one enters. Evagrius is often quoted as a spokesperson of the Orthodox tradition: "If you are a theologian, you will pray truly. And if you pray truly, you are a theologian."[9] Much ink has been spilled on the results of prayer, the types of prayer, the mechanics of prayer, its importance in the life of the disciple, and so on. In accord with our aims in this section, we will not attempt to redo or review that material, which is developed in other excellent works.[10]

We must acknowledge our perpetual struggle with the practice of prayer. The problem for most of us is not that we are unconvinced of the power of prayer, although philosophical determinism may foment this in us, but rather that we do not pray as much as we would like or know we should. Laziness and busyness form part of the equation, as does the persistent presence of doubt, which prevents us from praying about that which really matters to us. Add to this the issues of information overload or analysis paralysis. There are so many good approaches to prayer and so much to cover in our prayers that we are afraid of beginning. In some ways, we are afraid of being novices. All that would be OK if our lackluster prayer lives were simply a no-harm, no-foul matter of neglect. But they are not. We recognize with the prophet Samuel that prayerlessness, in the face of much need for petition and intercession, is a sin (1 Sam 12.23).

Christians throughout the ages have sought to remedy prayerlessness by utilizing a daily schedule of fixed-hour prayer—divine offices. The roots of this practice lie in Judaism, marvelously exemplified by the psalmist who wrote, "Seven times a day do I praise You" (Ps 119:164). Phyllis Tickle offers a concise summary of the development of this pattern of prayer:

---

9. Evagrius Ponticus, *Chapters on Prayer*, 61.

10. One outstanding work is Foster, *Prayer*. Enthusiasts will also be encouraged to the biography of eminent prayers, such as George Muller. The works of E. M. Bounds are terrific, although one may be put off by his role as a chaplain in the Confederate army.

We do not know the hours that were appointed in the Psalm-ist's time for those prayers. By the turn of the era, however, the devout had come to punctuate their work day with prayers on a regimen that followed the flow of Roman commercial life. Forum bells began the work day at six in the morning (prime, or first hour), sounded mid-morning break at nine (*terce*, or third hour), the noon meal and siesta or break at twelve (*sext*, or sixth hour), the re-commencing of trade at three (none, or ninth hour), and the close of business at six (vespers). With the addition of evening prayers and early prayers upon arising, the structure of fixed-hour prayer was established in a form that is very close to that which Christians still use today.[11]

Add to that pattern this helpful distinction from the late Donald Bloesch. He observed that when it comes to prayer, Christian traditions tend toward the poles of internal focus or external focus, which in this context he dubbed "mystical prayer" and "prophetic prayer."[12] In other words, presuming that we are not given to a dour fatalism, some of our prayer time ought to be focused on shaping ourselves and some on shaping the world around us. Indeed, this simple insight, coupled with the practice of fixed-hour prayer, gives us a way forward to creating a simple rule for our daily prayers.

We suggest beginning the day with *morning prayer*. This pray may be somewhat meditative, fostering a mindset of gratitude and contentment. As Matthew Henry has written, "the morning is the rudder of the day." This prayer may be enriched and centered by the slow, contemplative reading (*Lectio Divina*) of a psalm. Alternatively, one could spend a few minutes in silence, followed by a short entry in a gratitude diary. Our simple prayer rule also includes the *Prayer of Examen*, a powerful Jesuit/Ignatian form of prayer, typically undertaken at noon and at the close of day. In this prayer we first attune ourselves to God's presence, express gratitude, and then re-view our actions and emotions to that point. One of these elements will prompt us to prayer.

To those two types of prayer, we may add *evening prayers*. A help-ful structuring rubric for our evening prayers is ACTS, which stands for adoration, confession, thanksgiving, and supplication (intercession and petition). Our prayers of petition and intercession will be strengthened by keeping a small notebook. The notebook may contain a list of those we love, perhaps broken into seven groups, one per day of the week. This list, so organized, will remind us to intercede regularly on their behalf. The

11. Tickle, "Fixed-Hour Prayer."
12. Bloesch, *Struggle of Prayer*.

notebook may also contain a record of the concerns of the people who cross our paths. Perhaps you meet an atheist at the coffee shop, or a coworker tells you about troubles her kids are experiencing at school. Jot these down in your planner. This will give focus and clarity to your petitions and intercessions and will likely leave a strong impression on the people in your life as well. Before we begin our evening prayers, we will return to our journal to review the collected notes and experiences interpreted before entering a time of prayer.

The final practice of the core triad is fasting. Richard Foster, among others, argues that the most important text in all the Bible for establishing the importance of Christian fasting is Matthew 9:14–15:

> Then the disciples of John came to him, saying, "Why do we and the Pharisees fast, but your disciples do not fast?" And Jesus said to them, "Can the wedding guests mourn as long as the bridegroom is with them? The days will come when the bridegroom is taken away from them, and then they will fast."

Building on Foster, John Piper suggests that, in Jesus's mind, when he is taken away, that is, when he dies and ascends to the Father, his disciples will fast. They will do so, first and foremost, as an expression of their longing for the second coming of Christ. In short, while Jesus was here, the disciples didn't fast. When he is taken away, we fast. Fasting is a physical exclamation point at the end of the sentences: "I need you! I want you! I long for you! You are my treasure! I want more of you! Oh, for the day when you would return! Maranatha! Come, Lord Jesus!"[13] Hence, fasting, like the minimal elements of the Lord's Supper, points us to the eschatological feast that awaits Christ-followers. This, then, is the baseline meaning of a thick practice with multiple layers of significance.

It is difficult to overemphasize the role of fasting in the life of Jesus and hard to overstate the countercultural nature of this practice. When more than a third of Americans are overweight or obese, it becomes clear that we live in a milieu of gastronomic excess. Fasting forms a visible part of the spirituality of the Hebrew Bible and, as such, shaped the writers of the New Testament. Prolonged fasting, such as the fasts undertaken by Moses, Elijah, and Jesus, often precede special displays of God's majesty and power. Of course, a forty-day fast was an exceptional event in even their experience—never mind ours. While fasting must be more practicable than these heroic feats, the Matthew passage cited above, alongside other New Testament passages, seem to normalize the practice of fasting. To take one

---

13. Piper, "What Is the Purpose of Fasting?"

historical example, the eminent John Wesley required candidates for Methodist ordination to fast on Wednesdays and Fridays (the latter day carrying a connection with the day of crucifixion).

In this section, then, we have suggested that the practices of giving, prayer, and fasting form the core of our project of spiritual formation. This suggestion, moreover, flows not only from the teaching of Jesus, but from the example of the early church as illustrated in the *Teaching of the Twelve Apostles*, commonly referred to as the *Didache*.[14] This ancient text offers directives for each element of the core triad.

On fasting:

- "[Moreover] fast for those who persecute you" (1.3).

- "Before the baptism, moreover, the one who baptizes and the one being baptized must fast, and any others who can. And you must tell the one being baptized to fast for one or two days beforehand" 7.4.

- "Your fasts must not be identical with those of the hypocrites. They fast on Mondays and Thursdays; but you should fast on Wednesdays and Fridays" (8.1).[15]

On giving:

- "If someone strikes you 'on the right cheek, turn to him the other too, and you will be perfect.' If someone 'forces you to go one mile with him, go along with him for two'; if someone robs you 'of your overcoat, give him your suit as well.' If someone deprives you of your property, do not ask for it back. (You could not get it back anyway!) 'Give to everybody who begs from you and ask for no return'" (1.4–5)

- "Indeed, there is a further saying that relates to this: 'Let your donation sweat in your hands until you know to whom to give it'" (1.6)

- "Do not hesitate to give and do not give with a bad grace; for you will discover who He is that pays you back a reward with a good grace. Do not turn your back on the needy but share everything with your brother and call nothing your own. For if you have what is eternal in common, how much more should you have what is transient!" (4.7–8).

- "Say your prayers, give your charity, and do everything just as you find it in the gospel of our Lord" (15.4).

14. We are using the translation by Richardson in his *Early Christian Fathers*.

15. Some have read anti-Jewish sentiment into this injunction, but most likely the "hypocrites" in this context are Pharisees, since the *Didache* derives much from Matthew's gospel.

On prayer:

- "Do not hate anybody; but reprove some, pray for others, and still others love more than your own life" (2.7).

- "At the church meeting you must confess your sins, and not approach prayer with a bad conscience. That is the way of life" (4.14).

- "You should pray [in accord with the Our Father] three times a day" (8.3).

As soldiers of Christ, then, we have three basic practices which serve as weapons in our battle with sin. Like reading, writing, and arithmetic, they are to be learned early in our Christian life so that they then form the foundation upon which we employ additional weapons like *antirrhêtikos* or *talking back*.

Chapter 7

Antirrhêtikos or Talking Back

SAM HAMSTRA JR. WITH SAMUEL COCAR

We, your authors, serve Christ as pastors and professors. In our ministry contexts we repeatedly hear cries for relevance for the material we spew out. So, let us make it plain how we hope this project will help you, the reader, become more like Christ. Breaking it down as plainly as possible, we begin with the assumption that we who have been saved by grace through faith desire to love the Lord our God with heart, soul, mind, and strength, and to love our neighbor as we love ourselves. Motivated by love, we seek to become more and more like Christ, our Savior and Lord, by modeling the fruit of the Spirit with our lives. Motivated by that same love, we have responded to the call of Christ to serve him through a variety of vocations. We hope to do so faithfully with the help of the Holy Spirit, who not only dwells within us but works around us through many means, especially local congregations.

Not long after entering the road of discipleship, however, we discovered, like Paul, that we do what we don't want to do and don't do want we want to do. We step off the road for periods of time, some short and others so long that, in those moments, we describe ourselves as a "prodigal." Truth be told, our lack of faithfulness doesn't bother us much, especially if we keep away from the big sins with their significant social ramifications. Thankfully the Lord, who promised us an abundant life, breaks into our lives and calls us back to the road. He calls us to renew our covenant with him and, with the help of the Holy Spirit, to recommit ourselves to him. Hopefully, we find an opportunity to do just that each week as we gather with God's people.

Our experiences of being unfaithful have helped us discover typical sins or vices. With the help of those who have gone before us, we may categorize them as gluttony or hoarding, lust or impurity, avarice or greed, anger, sadness or dejection, acedia or listlessness, vainglory or vanity, and pride. Having named our enemy, we feel galvanized for spiritual warfare and burst onto the battlefield screaming, "Just say no!" But we can't just say no, for the enemy relentlessly assaults our individual and corporate vulnerabilities until we give in. Furthermore, blinded by our own biases and prejudices, both within us and within culture, we say yes to thoughts we fail to even recognize as temptations. We sin and don't even realize it.

The reason we pile one sin upon another is not a lack of desire. We can cry, mourn, and lament with the best of them. The reason we fall short in our devotion is a fundamental misunderstanding of the nature of sin. We think we can defeat sin by modifying our behavior when, in fact, we can only defeat sin at its root by defeating the thought which gives rise to sin. Sin begins with the spontaneous thoughts or *logismoi*. The thoughts function as suggestions or temptations and may be viewed as "symptoms of the vulnerability" of our human condition.[1] As such, they are not sin but may evolve into sin. They are the seed from which sin grows. Our spiritual progress, then, "depends on a close observation of the thoughts as they arise in the mind."[2] The work of observing thoughts will include categorizing each one into one of the eight *logismoi*. By so doing, we will be able to counter the thought with the appropriate response. Herein lies the benefit of discerning thoughts in community. The wisdom and insight of others can only help us with our propensity for self-deception. Here, for example, is a great insight from St. Philotheos of Sinai:

> It is by means of thoughts that the spirits of evil wage a secret war against the soul. For since the soul is invisible, these malicious powers naturally attack it invisibly. Both sides prepare their weapons, muster their forces, devise stratagems, clash in fearful battle, gain victories and suffer defeats. But this noetic warfare lacks one feature possessed by visible warfare: declaration of hostilities. Suddenly, with no warning, the enemy attacks

1. Tilby, *Seven Deadly Sins*, 59
2. Tilby, *Seven Deadly Sins*, 51.

the inmost heart, sets an ambush there, and kills the soul through sin. And for what purpose is this battle waged against us? To prevent us from doing God's will as we ask to do it when we pray "Thy will be done."[3]

Having identified the temptations in our minds, we have discovered that we best seek the Lord through prayer. Saint Gregory of Sinai once advised:

In the case of a beginner in the art of spiritual warfare. God alone can expel thoughts, for it is only those strong in such warfare who are in a position to wrestle with them and banish them. Yet even they do not achieve this by themselves, but they fight against them with God's assistance, clothed in the armor of His grace. So when thoughts invade you, in place of weapons call on the Lord Jesus frequently and persistently and then they will retreat; for they cannot bear the warmth produced in the heart by prayer and they flee as if scorched by fire. St John Klimakos tells us, "Lash your enemies with the name of Jesus," because God is a fire that cauterizes wickedness (cf. Deut 4:24; Heb 12:29). The Lord is prompt to help and will speedily come to the defense of those who wholeheartedly call on Him day and night (cf. Luke 18:7).[4]

Then we recommend putting to use our primary weapon—our sword (Eph 6:17). While the disciplined life fits us for spiritual battle, our primary weapon on the battlefield is the Word of God (Eph 6:17), utilized against our primary opponent—our thoughts or the *logismoi*, behind which lies Satan, the great adversary and accuser. Jesus modeled the martial art of fencing while face to face with Satan in the wilderness. Jesus wielded his sword by countering or talking back each thought raised by Satan with Scripture. Consequently, he left that battlefield victorious. We must do the same for, while we acknowledge with James K. A. Smith that we are what we love, it is also true that our loves are shaped by our thoughts.[5] So, if we hope that who we love shapes what we do, we best address our thoughts with the Word of God.

Again, if we hope to win the spiritual victory of loving faithfulness to our Lord, we best put our sword to use and talk back temptation with

3. Text 7 on inner and outer warfare from "Forty Texts on Watchfulness," in *Philokalia* 3.18–19.

4. Text 4 on how to expel thoughts from "On Prayer: Seven Texts," in *Philokalia* 4.277–78.

5. Smith, *Desiring the Kingdom*, ch. 1.

Scripture. We are not the first to suggest this. One of the more popular modern Christians to promote this practice is Joyce Meyer, whose *Battlefield of the Mind: Winning Battles in Your Mind* has sold more than four million copies.[6] Another is Kyle Winkler, who has even developed an app: "Shut Up, Devil!" is available free of charge at www.shutupdevil.org. But here we recommend the work of Evagrius Ponticus.

In his manual *Antirrhêtikos* (or *Talking Back*), Evagrius provides direction for Christ-followers on how to nip temptation in the bud by quoting specific Scripture passages back at it. By so doing, he encourages Christ-followers to follow the example of Christ, who, while tempted in the world, did the same. Evagrius promoted this approach to spiritual battle because he recognized that eradicating sinful behavior in our lives does not take place by dealing with symptoms as they manifest themselves in sinful behavior. Instead, it takes place by uprooting the seed that, left unchecked, develops into sinful behavior. As John Eudes Bamberger wrote:

> [We] cannot be perfected merely from action that proceeds from the exterior to the interior. [We] must be altered even in the depths of our spirits, where there lie hidden in the furthest recesses of our being unknown images, inaccessible to the external world save by some long-forgotten, distant paths which still exert their influence on [our] attitudes and ways.[7]

Clearly, the practice of talking back requires thorough knowledge of Scripture. The Word of God must be stored in our hearts, and the hearts of those with whom we share life in community, so that we may draw from that deep well of living water while in the midst of spiritual warfare. Evagrius provides hundreds of texts for us, but there are many more. The literal interpretation of many biblical passages speaks directly to specific temptations. The Sermon on the Mount, for example, addresses many thoughts faced daily by Christ-followers.

If we grant that Scripture may be interpreted allegorically, we will find countless others. The allegorical interpretation of the Bible, a popular approach to Scripture throughout the history of Christianity, especially in the centuries preceding the Reformation, assumes that the Bible has various levels of meaning and tends to focus on the spiritual sense. Evagrius excels in this hermeneutical method, one that provides space for the living Word of God to encourage us in the midst of our spiritual battles. One finds a modern example of this approach in the aforementioned work of Joyce Meyer. While we would not utilize this method in our attempts to understand and

---

6. The most recent edition was published by Faith Words in 2011.

7. From the Introduction to Evagrius Ponticus, *Praktikos*, xciii.

develop Christian doctrine, it is very useful for talking back temptation, as it opens up so much of Scripture, especially the Old Testament. Take, for example, the thought of acedia or sloth. Without labeling it as such, Meyer describes this temptation as giving up because faithfulness to our calling is just too hard. She writes,

> When I initially began to see from the Word of God how I was supposed to live and behave, and compared it to where I was, I was always saying, "I want to do things Your way, but it is too hard." That led me to Deuteronomy 30:11 in which He says that his commandments are not too difficult or too far away.[8]

The context of that passage is the renewal of the covenant between the Lord and the Israelites in Moab, a passage that includes numerous blessings and curses. Meyer essentially talked back the temptation of sloth with one verse among many from that important moment in the life of the Israelites. But then she took one more important step. She talked back with an additional Scripture, this one from the New Testament—allowing one passage of Scripture to interpret another. She writes, "The reason our Lord's commands are not too difficult for us is because He gives us His Spirit to work in us powerfully and to help us in all He has asked of us."[9] Meyer then repeats the exercise, this time noting that in Exodus 13:17 the Lord often prefers that his children take the hard way: "When Pharaoh let the people go, God led them not by the way of the Philistines, although that was nearer; for God said, 'Lest the people change their purpose when they see war and return to Egypt.'" She follows with, "You can be sure that anywhere the Lord leads you, He is able to keep you" (1 Cor 13:10).

Let us be clear at this moment that the spiritual weapon of talking back is not an end in and of itself. The ultimate outcome is the cultivation of virtue. Talking back, then, must be viewed as a weapon to be employed in battle with specific thoughts. By winning many battles, we win the war. John of Damascus describes the particular virtues that appear in our lives when we destroy the eight suggestions:

> Gluttony by self-control; unchastity by desire for God and longing for the blessings held in store; avarice by compassion for the poor; anger by goodwill and love for all men; worldly dejection by spiritual joy; listlessness by patience, perseverance and offering thanks to God; self-esteem by doing good in secret and by praying constantly with a contrite heart; and pride by not judging or

8. Meyer, *Battlefield of the Mind*, 199.
9. Meyer, *Battlefield of the Mind*, 199.

despising anyone in the manner of the boastful Pharisee (cf. Luke 18:11–12), and by considering oneself the least of all men.[10]

Suspicious Protestants, like ourselves, who view any talk of "working out our salvation" (Phil 2:12) as accommodation to works righteousness, notice that John of Damascus focuses not on salvation but on Christlikeness. He addresses the hope of all Christ-followers for spiritual transformation, not as a means by which to earn salvation but as a means to express our love for God and neighbor. At the same time, we remind ourselves that "the horse is made ready for battle, but victory rests with the Lord" (Prov 21:31).

Lest we err, we wrap up this surface level review of the spiritual weapon of *antirrhêtikos* (talking back) by clarifying several closely related concepts. First, we distinguish between thoughts and temptations. Margaret Funk writes that "the thoughts we find in our interior chatter cluster into eight themes which recur constantly . . . These thoughts are classic since they recur in every person of every era and cycle continuously."[11] Thankfully, not every thought cycling continuously through our minds functions as a temptation. Some thoughts just flow from observation and do not tempt us. We may think about some foods without being tempted by gluttony. We may imagine a particular person without vainglory or pride. We may enjoy the good gifts of God without being tempted by greed. However, we may refer to the thoughts which function as suggestions or temptations as *logismoi*. Their intent is to draw us into sin.

Second, we acknowledge that some thoughts function as temptations for some but not for others. One person may gain spiritual victory over a particular temptation and, in effect, defuse it. Another person may wrestle with the same temptation throughout his or her life. Take a simple example: thoughts arise about the weather. You may live and work in a context that is pretty much free from inclement weather. You don't think much of it. But if you live and work in a context that receives regular and moderate rain, the first and last thing you do each day is check the weather. Your observations about the weather, in turn, tempt you on more than one level. The same thought, then, tempts one but does not tempt another. In addition, the same thought may have tempted you years ago but not today. Years ago, a thought may have functioned like salt in a wound, but thanks to the work of the Holy Spirit, the wound has now become a scar and the thought doesn't function like a temptation. Such an experience gives us hope for victory over a particular temptation.

---

10. *Philokalia* 2.338.

11. Funk, *Thoughts Matter*, 20.

Third, we must state the obvious: thoughts rise in the mind. Some thoughts come and go. Others linger. When we ruminate on those that linger, the thoughts inevitably morph into temptations; when left unchecked, we will then yield to sin and vice. The mind, then, is the primary beginning place for all sin. It bears repeating. While we are what we love, our loves are shaped by our thoughts. The *logismoi*, then, may be understood as our primary opponent; they constitute the weapon by which demons present ungodly notions to Christians (especially monks), thereby attempting to draw us into sin. Take, for example, thoughts about food, which arise naturally in the course of a day. But in the hands of demons, they become temptations to a variety of sins, including gluttony. So understood, sin is not actually committed unless the Christ-follower succumbs by assenting to and embracing the temptation. "If the thought is allowed to persist, it leads the soul from merely thinking about sin to actually performing sin and thus to death."[12] If, however, Christ-followers repel the thought, they will be prevented from sinning. This means those "looking seriously for the right path on the spiritual journey" must engage the difficult work of renouncing thoughts, here understood as synonymous with temptations.[13]

Fourth, as Western Protestant Christians we would like to think that, as Spirit-filled Christ-followers, we might experience some level of spiritual transformation—Christlikeness—whereby certain thoughts no longer tempt us to sin. We hope to experience the "renewing of the mind" (Rom 12:1) and to grow "in the grace and knowledge of our Lord and Savior Jesus Christ" (2 Pet 3:18). After all, through Christ the old has passed away and the new has come (2 Cor 5:17) and we are being transformed by the Spirit "from one degree of glory to another" (2 Cor 3:18). We hope for the future described here by Cornelius van der Kooi and Gijsbert van den Brink:

> When we become aware that we see but little improvement in the passions and imaginations at the bottom of our heart, that nasty tendencies such as jealousy, hedonism, and superficiality seem to be more resilient than we thought, we can become more modest and realistic. If we acknowledge these things in ourselves rather than denying them, we will more consciously deal with them—for instance, by making a greater effort, based on our participation in Christ, to focus on what pleases God and is good for others. This pattern is what the gospel refers to as denying oneself: not disparaging feelings of always having to be submissive to

---

12. Brakke, "Introduction," 23, in Evagrius Ponticus, *Talking Back*.

13. Funk, *Thoughts Matter*, 9.

others, but the conscious choice, at different moments in life, to go the way of Christ and to be there for others.[14]

Or do the eight categories of thoughts reflect eight perpetual vulnerabilities in our born-again but broken beings as Christ-followers? Truth be told, we (your authors) do not have the answer to that question. We have not experienced sufficient spiritual transformation. We remain vulnerable to each of the eight thoughts. So, while in theory it appears possible to so mature in Christ that we are no longer tempted by one or more categories of thoughts—for the power of the resurrection dwells within us in the person of the Holy Spirit—that has not yet been our experience.[15] We will grant, however, that it has been possible to so grow in grace that a particular thought within a particular category no longer functions as a temptation. While a specific pastoral experience, like constant criticism and complaining, for example, used to encourage us to walk away from the ministry (acedia), we have learned—through talking back to the temptation—to find our identity, and root our call to ministry, in Christ. While the apparent success of others once triggered vainglory, we have been able to genuinely "rejoice with those who rejoice" (Rom 12:15).

---

14. Van der Kooi and Gijsbert van den Brink, *Christian Dogmatics*, 690.

15. See MacDonald, *Think Differently* for a more optimistic treatment on thought control.

Chapter 8

Excursus

Maximus Confessor

SAMUEL COCAR

It may help to provide a concrete example of the spirituality of the desert. We have already lifted up Evagrius Ponticus as the primary interlocutor in this conversation since he was a disciple of Origen and the most erudite contemplative and spiritual theologian to make his home in the deserts of Egypt and Palestine. Yet it is important to underscore that the connections between specific spiritual disciplines, virtues, and vices spread widely throughout the early monastic tradition. We find one example in the work of Maximus the Confessor.[1]

Maximus was born in Palestine in 580. As a young man, he served as a secretary for Emperor Heraclius until joining a monastery in 614, where he matured into "a thinker of uncommon brilliance, spiritual depth, courage, and sheer doggedness."[2] Those qualities served him well as he took on the great question of the divine and human nature in Christ. On the foundation of the Council of Chalcedon (451), Maximus vigorously affirmed what is now considered the orthodox position of the two wills (human and divine)

---

1. In the following paragraph we draw from the excellent work of Wilken, *First Thousand Years*, 283–87.

2. Wilken, *First Thousand Years*, 286.

of Christ. Those in power, however, disputed his teaching, which led to his arrest, conviction, condemnation, and exile.

> But the story does not end there. Even though he was con-
> demned for refusing to obey the imperial edict forbidding dis-
> cussion of the wills of Christ, Maximus continued to write and
> speak against the teaching of one will. So, he was brought out
> of evil to face yet another trial. This time his tormenters made
> sure he would neither write nor speak any more. The tongue
> that had taught two wills in Christ was ripped out of his mouth,
> and the hand that held the pen that defended the two wills was
> cut off. He was exiled to Lazica on the eastern shore of the Black
> Sea, where he died (662). Because of his witness to Christ un-
> der great suffering, he is remembered in Christian tradition as
> Maximus the Confessor.[3]

While Maximus dedicated considerable energy to defending the two natures of Christ as articulated by the Council of Chalcedon, he also served the church as an instructor in spiritual life. As a monk he provided detailed, practical guidance on how to live as a Christian, overcome our sinful passions, and truly love God and neighbor. Many of his writings are found in volume 2 of the *Philokalia*, including his *400 Chapters on Love*. In this work, Maximus articulates in winsome fashion the central aims and tools of the monastic vocation. We see that the ultimate goal of the renunciant's life is manifold: dispassion (or *apatheia*, 1.27), self-mastery, and love for G-d (2.1, 25). In Maximus' paradigm—which is, we argue, a wider patristic idiom—we engage in a battle to "acquire virtues and diminish the passions" (2.11). This battle is against impure thoughts (1.63) and against demons (2.31). Actually, the two shade into one another, since the demons wage war with us through our thoughts (1.91). Love is the ultimate end, as the spiritually perfect person "directs all affection to God" (3.98). Nevertheless, we acquire valuable "intermediate" virtues along the path toward mastery of the passions, including temperance and humility (1.80).

Maximus offers extensive counsel toward defeating impure thoughts and demons, beyond the mere employment of the martial analogy. For instance, love for God is generated by fasting, vigilance, psalmody, and prayer. Chastity and holiness likewise derive from psalmody, prayer, fasting, and vigils (1.42, 45). The demon of fornication is repulsed by fasting, hard work, vigils, solitude, and consistent prayer (2.19). The renunciant looking to halt the growth of strong desires (concupiscence) should turn to fasting, hard labor, and vigils; solitude, contemplation, prayer, and the desire for God

---

3. Wilken, *First Thousand Years*, 286–87.

will destroy it utterly (2.47). Similarly, anger can be checked by patience and meekness, which are its opposite virtues; anger is ultimately defeated by love, benevolence, and almsgiving. Almsgiving both reflects and cultivates love for others, which heals our irascible tendencies, while fasting nurtures self-control and heals our inordinate desires. These are completed by prayer, which purifies the mind (1.79).

Maximus' proffered remedies for certain impure thoughts and vices suggest a deep concern for the disposition of the body and the physical environment (see 2.92). Fasting is the antithesis of gluttony, "the mother and nurse of fornication" (1.81). Elsewhere he notes that excessive eating leads to intemperance, just as greed and vainglory lead to hatred (3.7). We also cannot hope ultimately to achieve dispassion if we do not abide by outward simplicity of lifestyle (1.27).

Maximus offers a number of frameworks and relationships for better understanding ourselves and the spiritual pilgrimage we travel. For instance, there exists a cyclical, self-reinforcing relationship between prayer and freedom from passion (3.42). Unfortunately, this is also true of greed and vainglory (3.83). Maximus offers us several maps of Christian progress. Obedience to the commandments progresses to self-control, which reaches its telos in *apatheia* (2.87). Again, invoking the distinction between concupiscible and irascible transgressions, Maximus remarks that the love of God opposes lust, and the love of neighbor opposes anger (4.75). Another "ladder" of spiritual perfection can be found in 4.91: the "correct use of things" leads to purity, which in turn yields discernment and finally detachment. The warrior advises us: "virtue sustained kills the passions, but virtue neglected rouses them anew" (4.54).

The chapters reinforce several of the points made thus far: the desert fathers tend to conflate demons and impure thoughts; the fathers are apt to draw martial analogies about the Christian life, since this was central to their experience of the desert; and finally, the fathers draw clear relationships not only between virtues and vices (e.g., greed and vainglory reinforce one another; humility halts anger), but also between disciplines and spiritual outcomes (e.g., almsgiving shows love and destroys anger; fasting strengthens self-control and destroys lust). The particulars of the spiritual landscape may differ from theologian to theologian, but the overall geography is remarkably similar. The desert fathers affirm with one voice that the Christian life is a battle in which impure thoughts suggested to us may become sinful deeds exercised by us. What must intervene is not mere good intentions, but a set of proper tools and armaments wielded by warriors trained in their use.

Chapter 9

Facing the Logismoi in Combat

SAM HAMSTRA JR. WITH SAMUEL COCAR

In this final section, we provide examples of *antirrhêtikos* or *talking back* from the desert tradition. We also allow the anecdotes and counsels of the monks to speak largely for themselves. So vital and sharp are the words of the desert fathers and their disciples that we benefit from removing the barriers between their wisdom and our lives. Before proceeding to their wisdom, a brief prologue is in order.

First, the reader ought not to be too disappointed that this stream of patristic wisdom comes to us largely in aphorisms. To the modern mind, unacquainted with the "sayings" form, or *verba*, it may appear disjointed, leading us to wonder at the theological system behind them. To be sure, the desert fathers tradition includes systematists, especially visible in the theological lineage of Origen, Evagrius, and Cassian (who were connected as well to the great Cappadocian fathers). The *primary* bearer of the desert patristic tradition, however, is the "saying" (*apopthegmata* or *verba*). This is how we encounter Abbas Macarius, Agatho, and Poemen—quite different from our experience of theologians like Barth, Edwards, or Schleiermacher.

Second, it bears repeating that the fathers are probably more attentive to the relationship between the details of our bodies for both worship and discipleship. We tend to act as if the body were irrelevant to our relationships with God and others. The fathers were all too aware of how bodily circumstances mischievously bound themselves up with our spiritual lives. Fasting, for example, was not only a direct counterstrike to the temptation of gluttony, but a regular regimen that also kept sexual temptation in check. St. Seraphim of Sarov, writing much later, wrote that "it is impossible to see visions of God on a full stomach." In any event, one best remember that, in most cases, the abbas and ammas offer concrete pastoral and spiritual direction, not grand theories of spiritual formation.

Third, we recommend that the reader, either in isolation or preferably within a small group that includes some veterans in the faith, develop a short list of thoughts for each of the eight sections. Remember, *Antirrhêtikos* was written for monks. But what would it look like if written for pastors? Or for academics? Or for truck drivers? Or homemakers? You name the group knowing that each one faces the *logismoi* but also knowing that the specific thoughts which rise in the minds of one group of people may differ from those that rise in the minds of another group, and both may differ from those who lived in the desert centuries ago, who did not have to wrestle with, as one example, the correlation between the desire to post on social media and pride. So share your temptations and, instead of talking about personal vulnerabilities, which should be taken for granted, dig into God's Word and together discover passages from Scripture that may be used to defeat the temptation time and time again.

We now proceed to anecdotes of the desert fathers and their disciples. We will follow the traditional framework of the desert fathers, who categorized spiritual temptations under eight thoughts. For the reader's edification, we will begin each thought with a description of that thought by Evagrius. The description will be taken from his *Praktikos*, which includes one hundred numerated chapters or paragraphs.[1] The *Praktikos*, one of Evagrius' most popular works, deals with the ascetic life but also has much to say about prayer and about "the work of cleansing the affections of passionate and disordered impulses."[2] Then we will add to each section a selection from *Antirrhêtikos*.[3] In this volume, Evagrius describes the eight kinds of temptations or *logismoi*. Each category includes many thoughts. Under the thought of gluttony, for example, Evagrius identified sixty-nine thoughts that may lead to the sin of gluttony. Evagrius then coupled each

1. We will quote Evagrius Ponticus, *Praktikos*, translated by Bamberger, 17–20.

2. Bamberger, Introduction to Evagrius Ponticus, *Praktikos*, lix.

3. References that follow will be taken from Evagrius Ponticus, *Talking Back*, translated by David Brakke.

thought with a passage of Scripture that the Christ-follower may employ while talking back to the thought. The work includes 487 couplets. Finally, we will add counsels from the *Philokalia*, several collections of sayings, and from the *Institutes*[4] by John Cassian. As noted earlier, the *Philokalia* collects writings mostly centering on practicing the virtues and spiritual living in a monastery. The collection was compiled in the eighteenth century by St. Nikodemos of the Holy Mountain and St. Makarios of Corinth. Also, as noted earlier, the *Sayings* or the *Apophthegmata Patrum* is a collection of the writings of some of the early desert monks and nuns, the best known of which was Anthony the Great, who moved to the desert in 270–271 and became known as the father and founder of desert monasticism. They are still in print as *Sayings of the Desert Fathers*.[5]

ON FACING GLUTTONY

Praktikos

> Chapter 7: The thought of gluttony suggests to the monk that he give up his ascetic efforts in short order. It brings to his mind concern for his stomach, for his liver and spleen, the thought of a long illness, scarcity of the commodities of life and finally of his edematous body and the lack of care by the physicians. These things are depicted vividly before his eyes. It frequently brings him to recall certain ones among the brethren who have fallen upon such sufferings. There even comes a time when it persuades those who suffer from such maladies to visit those who are practicing a life of abstinence and to expose their misfortune and relate how these came about as a result of the ascetic life.[6]

Antirrhêtikos

> Thought 4: Against the thought that seeks to be filled with food and drink and gives no heed to the harm that springs from filling the belly: *Having eaten and been filled, pay attention to*

---

4. The full title of this work, as translated into the English, is *The Twelve Books on the Institutes of the Coenobia and the Remedies for the Eight Principal Faults*. We will draw from the online version made available by *Documenta Catholica Omni*.

5. We will draw from https://www.patristics.co/sayings/.

6. Evagrius Ponticus, *Praktikos* 7.

yourself, lest you forget the Lord your God, who brought you out of the land of Egypt, out of the house of slavery (Deut 6:11–12).

Thought 16: Against the thought that is anxious about food and drink and diligent about where it can get them: *Cast your anxiety upon the Lord, and he will sustain you* (Ps 54:22).[7]

Thought 28: Against the thought that hinders us by suggesting that we not give from our bread to those in need and by saying to me, "That person can [find mercy] anywhere, but we cannot approach any stranger's door:" *The one who shows mercy will himself be supported, for he gave to the poor from his own bread* (Prov 22:9).

Thought 46: Against the soul that at the time of attack wants to find strong armor: *Then Jesus was led up by the Spirit into the wilderness to be tempted by the devil. He fasted forty days and forty nights, and afterwards he was famished* (Matt 4:1–2).

Thought 47: Against the thoughts that are anxious about food and clothing on the pretexts of hospitality, illnesses, and prolonged miseries of the body: *Do not worry about your life, what you will eat or what you will drink, or about your body, what you will wear. Is not life more than food, and the body more than clothing?* (Matt 6:25).

St. Diadochos of Photiki, *On Spiritual Knowledge and Discrimination: One Hundred Texts*

43: Those pursuing the spiritual way should train themselves to hate all uncontrolled desires until this hatred becomes habitual. With regard to self-control in eating, -we must never feel loathing for any kind of food, for to do so is abominable and utterly demonic. It is emphatically not because any kind of food is bad in itself that we refrain from it. But by not eating too much or too richly we can to some extent keep in check the excitable parts of our body. In addition, we can give to the poor what remains over, for this is the mark of sincere love.[8]

7. Note that the desert tradition employed the numbering system of the Septuagint, which differs by one from that employed today. In this case, their Psalm 54 is our Psalm 55.

8. From *Philokalia* 1:266.

John Cassian, *Institutes*

Book 5, chapter 6: The belly when filled with all kinds of food gives birth to seeds of wantonness, nor can the mind, when choked with the weight of food, keep the guidance and government of the thoughts. For not only is drunkenness with wine wont to intoxicate the mind, but excess of all kinds of food makes it weak and uncertain, and robs it of all its power of pure and clear contemplation.

ON FACING LUST

Praktikos

Chapter 8: The demon of impurity impels one to lust after bodies. It attacks more strenuously those who practice continence, in the hope that they will give up their practice of this virtue, feeling that they gain nothing by it. This demon has a way of bowing the soul down to practices of an impure kind, defiling it, and causing it to speak and hear certain words almost as if the reality were actually present to be seen.

Antirrhêtikos

Thought 21: To the Lord concerning the multitude of unclean thoughts that trouble and afflict us and attract our intellect to diverse faces: *Lord, why are they who afflict me so numerous? Many rise up against me. Many say to my soul, "There is no salvation for him in his God." But you, Lord, are my helper, my glory, and the one who lifts up my head* (Ps 3:2–4).

Thought 27: To the Lord concerning the demon that suddenly fell upon the body, but could not conquer the intellect through the unclean thoughts that attacked it: *You have turned my sorrow into dace for me; you have ripped off my sackcloth and have girded me with gladness, so that my glory may sing praise to you and I may not be pierced* (Ps 29:12–13).

Thought 39: Against the unclean thought that entices us and turns us back to that sin for which we have many times repented before the Lord: *Just as a dog, when it returns to its own vomit, becomes abominable, so is a fool who returns in his wickedness to his own sin* (Prov 26:11).

Thought 51: To the Lord concerning the thoughts of fornication that have persisted in me: *See, Lord, my humiliation, for the enemy has become magnified* (Lam 1:9).

Thought 56: Against the intellect that, because of image of men and women that are established in its thinking, is eager to commit a sin: *Everyone who looks at a woman with lust has already committed adultery with her in his heart* (Matt 5:28).

St. Diodochas of Photiki, *Spiritual Knowledge and Discrimination*

Of course, this passion troubles men not only after they mature in the virtues, but also before that; in either case the soul is made to appear worthless, however great its virtues may be. We should fight (this) demon . . . by means of self-control, freedom from anger, and intense meditation on death, until we come to perceive unceasingly the energy of the Holy Spirit within us and rise with the Lord's help above even these passions.[9]

St. Neilos the Ascetic, *Ascetic Discourse*

Often the vice of unchastity has its first beginning in self-esteem; the gateway at the entrance appears attractive but hidden behind it lies the destructive path that leads the mindless into the realm of death. Under the influence of self-esteem, a man may perhaps enter the priesthood or the life of monastic perfection; and because many come to him for help, his self-esteem makes him think highly of himself thanks to what he says and does. So, by beguiling him with such thoughts, self-esteem draws him far away from the inner watchfulness that he should possess. Then it suggests to him that he should meet a woman of supposedly

9. *Philokalia* 1:259.

holy life, and so leads him to assent to an act of carnal lust, depriving his conscience of its intimate communion with God and plunging it into abject disgrace. To 'tie tail to tail' like Samson, let us reflect how this man's thought began and where it led him; and let us consider how he was punished for his self-esteem by falling into a shameful act of unchastity. Then we shall see clearly the contrast between the beginning and .the end, and the way they are linked together.[10]

John Cassian, *Institutes*

Book 6, chapter 5: If we really desire to enter into this spiritual combat on the same terms as the Apostle (2 Tim. 4:7), let us concentrate our every effort at dominating this unclean spirit by placing our confidence not in our own forces but on the help of God. Human effort will never be able to win through here. For the soul will be attacked by this vice as long as it does not recognize that it is in a war beyond its powers and that it cannot obtain victory by its own effort unless it is shored up by the help and protection of the Lord.[11]

ON FACING SORROW OR DEJECTION

Praktikos

Chapter 10: Sadness tends to come up at times because of the deprivation of one's desires. On other occasions it accompanies anger. When it arises from the deprivation of desires it takes place in the following manner. Certain thoughts first drive the soul to the memory of home and parents, or else to that of one's former life. Now when these thoughts find that the soul offers no resistance but rather follows after them and pours itself out in pleasures that are still only mental in nature, they then seize her and drench her in sadness, with the result that these ideas she was just indulging no longer remain. In fact they cannot be had in reality, either, because of her present way of life. So the

---

10. *Philokalia* 1:226–27.

11. Kardong translation.

miserable soul is now shriveled up in her humiliation to the degree that she poured herself out upon these thoughts of hers.[12]

Antirrhêtikos

Thought 1: Against the soul that, due to the sadness that comes upon it, thinks that the Lord has not heard its groaning: *The children of Israel groaned because of their tasks, and cried, and their cry because of their tasks went up to God. And God heard their groanings* (Exod 2:23–24).

Thought 17: Against the soul that wants to know the reason for these trials . . . *so that he might afflict you and test you and treat you well at the end of your days* (Deut 8:16).

Thought 40: Against the soul that, in the time of sadness, wants to find in prayer spiritual words: *Do not forsake me, Lord; my God, do not depart from me. Come near to help me, Lord of my salvation* (Ps 37:22–23).

Thought 67: Against the soul that does not understand that weakness of faith brings trepidation and fear into the heart: *Do not let your hearts be troubled. Have faith in God, have faith also in me* (John 14:1).

Thought 71: Against the souls thought that supposes that it is tested beyond its strength: *God is faithful, and he will not let you be tested beyond your strength, but with the testing he will also provide the way out so that you may be able to endure it* (1 Cor 10:13).

John Cassian, *On the Eight Vices*[13]

A man can be harmed by another only through the causes of the passions which lie within himself. It is for this reason that God, the Creator of all and the Doctor of men's souls, who alone has accurate knowledge of the soul's wounds, does not tell us to forsake the company of men; He tells us to root out the causes of

12. Evagrius Ponticus, *Praktikos* 10.
13. *Philokalia* 1:87–88.

evil within us and to recognize that the soul's health is achieved not by a man's separating himself from his fellows, but by his living the ascetic life in the company of holy men. When we abandon our brothers for some apparently good reason, we do not eradicate the motives for dejection but merely exchange them, since the sickness which lies hidden within us will show itself again in other circumstances.

ON FACING AVARICE OR GREED

Praktikos

Chapter 9: Avarice suggests to the mind a lengthy old age, inability to perform manual labor (at some future date), famines that are sure to come, sickness that will visit us, the pinch of poverty, the great shame that comes from accepting the necessities of life from others.[14]

Antirrhêtikos

Thought 5: Against the thought of love of money that withheld compassion from a brother who asked out of his need and that advised us to store up for ourselves alone: *You shall love your neighbor as yourself. I am the Lord* (Lev 19:18).

Thought 9: Against the thought that did not permit us to give to a needy brother who asked to borrow something from us: *You shall not close your hand to your brother who is in need. You shall open your hands to him and lend him as much as he needs* (Deut 15:7–8).

Thought 21: Against the thoughts that meditate upon riches and give no heed to the consuming pain of wealth: *If wealth should increase, do not set your heart upon it* (Ps 61:11).

Thought 27: Against the soul that because of the passion of love of money offers scarcely anything for mercy: *Let not mercy and faith forsake you, but bind them about your neck, and you will find favor. Provide good things before the Lord and human beings* (Prov 3:3–4).

14. Evagrius Ponticus, *Praktikos* 9.

Thought 44: Against the thought that did not permit us to share our wealth when a noble occasion was depicted before our eyes: *How hard it will be for those who have wealth to enter the kingdom of God!* (Mark 10:23).

Sayings of the Fathers—Isidore[15]

3: He also said that for forty years he had been tempted to sin in thought but that he had never consented either to covetousness or to anger.

4: He also said, "When I was younger and remained in my cell I set no limit to prayer; the night was for me as much the time of prayer as the day."

Mark the Ascetic, *On the Spiritual Law: Two Hundred Thoughts*

165: Reject all thoughts of greed, and you will be able to see the devil's tricks.[16]

John Cassian, *Institutes*

Book 7, chapter 6: Wherefore not this evil seem of no account or unimportant to anybody: for as it can easily be avoided, so if it has once got hold of any one, it scarcely suffers him to get at the remedies for curing it. For it is a regular nest of sins, and a "root of all kinds of evil," and becomes a hopeless incitement to wickedness, as the Apostle says, "Covetousness," i.e. the love of money, "is a root of all kinds of evil."

15. Isidore was a monk of Scetis and early companion of Macarius. He is mentioned by Cassian as one of the heads of the four communities in Scetis.

16 From *Philokalia* 1:121.

ON FACING ANGER

Praktikos

Chapter 11: The most fierce passion is anger. In fact it is defined as a boiling and stirring up of wrath against one who has given injury—or is thought to have done so. It constantly irritates the soul and above all at the time of prayer it seizes the mind and flashes the picture of the offensive person before one's eyes. Then there comes a time when it persists longer, is transformed into indignation, stirs up alarming experiences by night. This is succeeded by a general debility of the body, malnutrition with its attendant pallor, and the illusion of being attacked by poisonous wild beasts. These four last mentioned consequences following upon indignation may be found to accompany many thoughts.[17]

Antirrhêtikos

Thought 2: Against the thought of anger that arise along the way of righteous living: *Do not get angry along the way* (Gen 45:24).

Thought 23: Against the thought of anger that prevents us from answering with humility those who chastise us rightly: *Anger destroys even wise persons; a submissive answer turns away anger, but a painful word raises up anger* (Prov 15:1).

Thought 32: Against the thought that provokes me to write to the person who has caused us trouble harmful words that will strike his heart: *Woe to those who write evil, for it I by writing that they write evil* (Isa 10:1).

Thought 35: Against the thought that is agitated against a brother due to listlessness: *If you are angry with a brother, you will be liable to judgment* (Matt 5:22).

Thought 42: Against the thought that holds a grudge and endeavors to repay evil to the one who grieved it: *Do not repay evil for evil, but take thought for what is noble in the sight of all* (Rom 12:17).

---

17. Evagrius Ponticus, *Praktikos* 11.

Saint Isaiah the Solitary, *On Guarding the Intellect*

There is among the passions an anger of the intellect, and this anger is in accordance with nature. Without anger a man cannot attain purity: he has to feel angry with all that is sown in him by the enemy. When Job felt this anger he reviled his enemies, calling them 'dishonorable men of no repute, lacking everything good, whom I would not consider fit to live with the dogs that guard my flocks' (cf. Job 30:1, 4. LXX). He who wishes to acquire the anger that is in accordance with nature must uproot all self-will, until he establishes within himself the state natural to the intellect.[18]

Sayings of the Desert (Mothers)—Syncletica[19]

13. She also said, "It is good not to get angry, but if this should happen, the Apostle does not allow you a whole day for this passion, for he says: 'Let not the sun go down.'" (Eph 4.25) Will you wait till all your time is ended? Why hate the man who has grieved you? It is not he who has done the wrong, but the devil. Hate sickness but not the sick person.

John Cassian, *Institutes*

Book 8, chapter 17: The chief part then of our improvement and peace of mind must not be made to depend on another's will, which cannot possibly be subject to our authority, but it lies rather in our own control. And so the fact that we are not angry ought not to result from another's perfection, but from our own virtue, which is acquired, not by somebody else's patience, but by our own long-suffering.

18. From *Philokalia* 1:22.

19. Syncletica of Alexandria, a Christian saint and desert mother of the fourth century. With her younger sister Syncletica, she abandoned city life and chose to reside in a crypt adopting as a hermit. Her life gained the attention of many women came to live as her disciples in Christ.

ON FACING ACEDIA OR LISTLESSNESS

Praktikos

The demon of acedia—also called the noonday demon—is the one that causes the most serious trouble of all. He presses his attack upon the monk about the fourth hour and besieges the soul until the eighth hour. First of all he makes it seem that the sun barely moves, if at all, and that the day is fifty hours long. Then he constrains the monk to look constantly out the windows, to walk outside the cell, to gaze carefully at the sun to determine how for it stands from the ninth hour,[20] to look now this way and now that to see if perhaps one of the brethren appears from his cell. Then too he instills in the heart of the monk a hatred for the place, a hatred for his very life itself, a hatred for manual labor. He leads him to reflect that charity has departed from among the brethren, that there is no one to give encouragement. Should there be someone at this period who happens to offend him in some way or other, this too the demon uses to contribute further to his hatred. This demon drives him along to desire other sites where he can more easily procure life's necessities, more readily find work and make a real success of himself. He goes on to suggest that, after all, it is not the place that is the basis of pleasing the Lord, God is to be adored every- where. He joins to these reflections the memory of his dear ones and of his former way of life. He depicts life stretching out for a long period of time, and brings before the mind's eye the toil of ascetic struggle and, as the say has it, leaves no leaf unturned to induce the monk to forsake his cell and drop out of the fight. No other demon follows close upon the heels of this one (when he is defeated) but only a state of deep peace and inexpressible joy arrive out of this struggle.[21]

Antirrhêtikos

Thought 12: Against the thoughts of acedia that take away my hope: *I believe that I will see the good things of the Lord in the land of the living* (Ps 26:13).

---

20. The ninth hour (3 p.m.) was dinner time.
21. Evagrius Ponticus, *Praktikos* 12.

Thought 20: Against the soul that succumbs to acedia and be-comes filled with thoughts of sadness: *Why are you sad, my soul? And why do you trouble me? Hope in God, for I will give thanks to him, the salvation of my countenance and my God* (Ps 41:6).

Thought 37: Against the soul that has fallen under the weight of acedia and cries out due to the sloth that results from thoughts of acedia: *Look, all those who oppose you will be put to shame and confounded, for they will be as if they were not, and all your opponents will perish* (Isa 41:11).

Thought 48: Against the thoughts that due to acedia dare to murmur: *Do not complain as some of them did, and were de-stroyed by the destroyer* (1 Cor 10:10).

Thought 56: Against the thought of the soul that is saddened because of the spirit of acedia that has persisted in it and altered its condition: *My brothers, whenever you face trails of any kind, consider it nothing but joy, because you know that the testing of your faith produces endurance; and let endurance have its full ef-fect, so that you may be mature and complete, lacking in nothing* (Jas 1:2–4).

Sayings of the Desert (Mothers)—Syncletica

27: She also said, "There is grief that is useful, and there is grief that is destructive. The first sort consists in weeping over one's own faults and weeping over the weakness of one's neighbors, in order not to destroy one's purpose, and attach oneself to the per-fect good. But there is also a grief that comes from the enemy, full of mockery, which some call accidie. This spirit must be cast out, mainly by prayer and psalmody."

Sayings of the Desert Fathers—Abba Makarios [22]

When I was a young man, assailed by [acedia] in my cell, I went out to the desert, saying to myself: "Put a question to

22. From Wortley, trans., ed., *Anonymous Sayings of the Desert Fathers*, N490. Macarius the Great (the Egyptian), born c. 300, was ordained priest and lived as an anchorite in a village until he was falsely blamed for the pregnancy of a girl there; when

whomsoever you meet to gain some benefit." Coming across a lad herding oxen I said to him: "What am I to do, boy, for I'm hungry." "Eat then," he told me. Again I spoke: "I have eaten and I am still hungry," to which he again replied: "Well, eat again." Again I said: "I had eaten many times and am hungry again," then he said to me: "Perhaps you are an ass, abba, because you want to be always munching." Somewhat edified, I went my way.

John Cassian, *On the Eight Vices*

It is also good to recall what Abba Moses, one of the most experienced of the fathers, told me. I had not been living long in the desert when I was troubled by listlessness. So I went to him and said: "Yesterday I was greatly troubled and weakened by listlessness, and I was not able to free myself from it until I went to see Abba Paul." Abba Moses replied to me by saying: "So far from freeing yourself from it, you have surrendered to it completely and become its slave. You must realize that it will attack all the more severely because you have deserted your post, unless from now on you strive to subdue it through patience, prayer and manual labor."[23]

ON FACING VAINGLORY

Praktikos

Chapter 13: The spirit of vainglory is most subtle and it readily grows up in the souls of those who practice virtue. It leads them to desire to make their struggles known publicly, to hunt after the praise of men. This in turn leads to their illusory healing of women, or to their hearing fancied sounds as the cries of the demons—crowds of people who touch their cloths. This demon predicts besides that they will attain to the priesthood. It has men knocking at the door, seeking audience with them. If the monk does not willingly yield to their request, he is bound and led away. When in this way he is carried aloft by vain hope, the demon vanishes and the monk is left to be tempted by the

---

he was cleared, he went to Scetis. He died in 390.

23. From *Philokalia* 1:90–91.

demon of pride or of sadness who brings upon thoughts opposed to his hopes. It also happens at times that a man who a short while before was a holy priest, is led off bound and is handed over to the demon of impurity to be sifted by him.[24]

Antirrhêtikos

Thought 2: Against the thought of vainglory that stirs up in me jealousy toward the bothers who have received from the Lord the gift of knowledge: *Are you jealous of me? Would that all the Lord's people were given to be prophets when the Lord gives his Spirit upon them* (Num 11:29).

Thought 6: Against the thought of vainglory, "Look, you are honored among all the brothers:" *I am a humble person and not honored* (1 Sam 18:23).

Thought 13: Against the thought that advised us before we have reached stability to preside over the brothers and lead their souls in the knowledge of Christ: *There is a way that seems to people to be right, but its ends lead to death* (Prov 14:12).

Thought 33: Against the thoughts of vainglory that compel the soul to speak in empty words, and that endeavor to entangle the intellect in transitory affairs, by which they set in motion in us either desire or anger, or that depicts in the intellect obscene visions that spoil the condition of purity that adorns and crowns our prayer: *I tell you, on the day of judgment you will have to give an account for every careless word you utter; for by your words you will be justified, and by your words you will be condemned* (Matt 12:36–37).

Thought 41: Against the thought of vainglory that encourages us to teach although we have not acquired the soul's health or knowledge of the truth: *Not many of you should become teachers, for you know that we who teach will be judged with strictness. For all of us make many mistakes. Anyone who makes no mistakes in speaking is perfect, able to keep the whole body in check with a bridle* (Jas 3:1–2).

---

24. Evagrius Ponticus, *Praktikos* 13.

Sayings of the Desert Fathers—Macarius

A brother came to see Abba Macarius the Egyptian, and said to him, "Abba, give me a word, that I may be saved." So the old man said, "Go to the cemetery and abuse the dead." The brother went there, abused them and threw stones at them; then he returned and told the old man about it. The latter said to him, "Didn't they say anything to you?" He replied, "No." The old man said, "Go back tomorrow and praise them." So the brother went away and praised them, calling them, "Apostles, saints and righteous men." He returned to the old man and said to him, "I have complimented them." And the old man said to him, "Did they not answer you?" The brother said no. The old man said to him, "You know how you insulted them and they did not reply, and how you praised them and they did not speak; so you too if you wish to be saved must do the same and become a dead man. Like the dead, take no account of either the scorn of men or their praises, and you can be saved."

Sayings of the Desert (Mothers)—Theodora[25]

5: The same Amma said that a teacher ought to be a stranger to the desire for domination, vain-glory, and pride; one should not be able to fool him by flattery, nor blind him by gifts, nor conquer him by the stomach, nor dominate him by anger; but he should be patient, gentle and humble as far as possible; he must be tested and without partisanship, full of concern, and a lover of souls.

John Cassian, *Institutes*

Book 11, chapter 5: Our elders admirably describe the nature of this malady as like that of an onion, and of those bulbs which When stripped of one covering you find to be sheathed m another; and as often as you strip them, you find them still protected.

---

25. Theodora of Alexandria was a desert mother married to a prefect of Egypt. In order to perform penance for a sin she committed, she disguised herself as a man and joined a monastery in Thebaid. Her true identity as a woman was discovered only after her death.

ON FACING PRIDE

Praktikos

Chapter 14: The demon of pride is the cause of the most damaging fall for the soul. For it induces the monk to deny that God is his helper and to consider that he himself is the cause of virtuous actions. Further, he gets a big head in regard to the brethren, considering them stupid because they do not all have this same opinion of him. Anger and sadness follow on the heels of this demon, and last of all there comes in its train the greatest of maladies—derangement of mind, associated with wild ravings and hallucinations of whole multitudes of demons in the sky.[26]

Antirrhêtikos

Thought 13: Against the soul that proudly supposes that by its own strength it has conquered the demons that oppose our doing the commandments: *Do not say in your heart, "My strength and the might of my hand have made for me this great power." But you shall remember the Lord your God, who gives you the strength* (Deut 8:17–18).

Thought 30: Against the thought of pride that glorifies me on the pretext that I edify souls with a stable way of life and knowledge of God: *Unless the Lord builds the house, the builders labor in vain; unless the Lord guards the city, the guards keep watch in vain* (Ps 126:1).

Thought 52: Against the proud thought that justifies itself and is not pleased by what is accomplished by the brothers in weakness: *For all who exalt themselves will be humbled, and those who humble themselves will be exalted* (Luke 14:11).

Thought 55: Against the proud thought that glorifies me on the pretext "I am able not only not to be enslaves to the belly, but also to conquer anger": *It was not I, but the grace of God that is with me* (1 Cor 15:10).

---

26. Evagrius Ponticus, *Praktikos* 14.

Thought 59: Against the proud thought that exalts me on the pretext that there is no image of sin in my thinking: *If we say that we have no sin, we deceive ourselves, and the truth is not in us. If we confess our sins, he who is faithful and just will forgive our sins and cleanse us from all unrighteousness* (1 John 1:8–9).

Sayings of the Desert Fathers—Abba Anthony[27]

7: Abba Anthony said, 'I saw the snares that the enemy spreads out over the world and I said groaning, "What can get through from such snares?" Then I heard a voice saying to me, "Humility."

John Cassian, *Institutes*

Book 13, chapter 9: And so we can escape the snare of this most evil spirit, if in the case of every virtue in which we feel that we make progress, we say these words of the Apostle: "Not I, but the grace of God with me," and "by the grace of God I am what I am;" and "it is God that worketh in us both to will and to do of His good pleasure."

27. Anthony the Great, called "The Father of Monks," was born in central Egypt about 251 AD, the son of peasant farmers who were Christian. He died at the age of 105. His biography, written by Athanasius, was very influential in spreading the ideals of monasticism throughout the Christian world.

Bibliography

Amesbury, Richard. "Fideism." In *The Stanford Encyclopedia of Philosophy*, edited by Edward N. Zalta. Fall 2017 ed. http://plato.stanford.edu/entries/fideism/.

Augustine. *Confessions*. Translated by R. S. Pine-Coffin. London: Penguin, 1961.

Barker, Margaret. *The Lost Prophet: The Book of Enoch and its Influence on Christianity*. Sheffield, UK: Sheffield Phoenix, 2005.

Barton, Ruth Haley. *Pursuing God's Will Together: A Discernment Practice for Leadership Groups*. Downers Grove, IL: InterVarsity, 2012.

Beilby, James K., and Paul Rhodes Eddy, eds. *Understanding Spiritual Warfare: Four Views*. Grand Rapids: Baker, 2012.

Boyd, Gregory A. *God at War: The Bible and Spiritual Conflict*. Downers Grove, IL: InterVarsity, 1997.

Bloesch, Donald. *The Crisis of Piety*. Grand Rapids: Eerdmans, 1968.

———. *The Holy Spirit: Works & Gifts*. Downers Grove, IL: InterVarsity, 2000.

———. *The Struggle of Prayer*. Colorado Springs, CO: Helmers & Howard, 1988.

Brakke, David. *Demons and the Making of the Monk: Spiritual Combat in Early Christianity*. Cambridge, MA: Harvard University Press, 2009.

Brooks, David. *The Road to Character*. New York: Random House, 2015.

Buechner, Frederick. *Beyond Words: Daily Readings in the ABC's of Faith*. San Francisco: HarperCollins, 2004.

Bullock, C. Hassell. *An Introduction to the Old Testament Prophetic Books*. Chicago: Moody, 2007.

Calhoun, Adele Ahlberg. *Spiritual Disciplines Handbook: Practices that Transform Us*. Rev. ed. Downers Grove, IL: Intervarsity, 2015.

Cary, Phillip. *Good News for Anxious Christians: Ten Practical Things You Don't Have to Do*. Grand Rapids: Brazos, 2010.

Charles, Robert, trans. *The Apocrypha and Pseudepigrapha of the Old Testament*. Oxford: Clarendon, 1913.

Clément, Olivier. *The Roots of Christian Mysticism: Texts from the Patristic Era with Commentary*. 2nd ed. Hyde Park, NY: New City, 2013.

Cone, Orello. "The Pauline Doctrine of Sin." *American Journal of Theology* 2/2 (1898) 241–67.

Cushman, Philip. "Why the Self Is Empty: Toward a Historically Situated Psychology." *American Psychologist* 45/5 (1990) 599–611.

DeYoung, Rebecca Konyndyk. *Glittering Vices: A New Look at the Seven Deadly Sins and Their Remedies.* Grand Rapids: Brazos, 2009.

———. "Glorious Things of Me Are Spoken: The Vice of Vainglory." Calvin Institute of Christian Worship. August 11, 2016. https://worship.calvin.edu/resources/resource-library/glorious-things-of-me-are-spoken-the-vice-of-vainglory/.

———. *Vainglory: The Forgotten Vice.* Grand Rapids: Eerdmans, 2014.

Documenta Catholica Omni. Cooperatorum Veritatis Societas. http://www.documentacatholicaomnia.eu.

Durant, Will. *The Story of Philosophy: The Lives and Opinions of the World's Greatest Philosophers.* New York: Simon & Schuster, 1965.

Edwards, Jonathan. *The Religious Affections.* Carlisle, PA: Banner of Truth, 1961.

Epictetus. *The Art of Living: The Classical Manual on Virtue, Happiness, and Effectiveness.* Translated by Sharon Lebell. San Francisco: HarperCollins, 1994.

Evagrius Ponticus. *The Praktikos & Chapters on Prayer.* Translated John Eudes Bamberger. Collegeville, MN: Cistercian, 1972.

———. *Talking Back: A Monastic Handbook for Combating Demons.* Translated by David Brakke. Collegeville, MN: Cistercian, 2009.

Foster, Richard J. *Prayer: Finding the Heart's True Home.* San Francisco: HarperCollins, 2002.

Funk, Mary Margaret. *Thoughts Matter: The Practice of the Spiritual Life.* New York: Continuum, 1988.

Guardini, Romano. *Learning the Virtues that Lead You to God.* Rev. ed. Manchester, NH: Sophia Institute, 1987.

House, Paul R., and Eric Mitchell. *Old Testament Survey.* 2nd ed. Nashville: Broadman & Holman, 2007.

Howard, Evan B. *Introduction to Christian Spirituality.* Grand Rapids: Brazos, 2008.

Janzen, Waldemar. *Old Testament Ethics: A Paradigmatic Approach.* Louisville: Westminster John Knox, 1994.

John Cassian. *John Cassian, The Institutes.* Translated by Boniface Ramsey. Mahwah, NJ: Paulist, 2000.

———. *Institutes by St. John Cassian.* Translated by Terrance G. Kardong. Mahwah, NJ: Paulist, 2000.

Johnson, Robert Francis. "Achan." In *The Interpreter's Dictionary of the Bible*, edited by Keith Crim et al., 1:26. Nashville: Abingdon, 1976.

Keenan, James F. *Virtues for Ordinary Christians.* London: Sheed & Ward, 1996.

Keller, David G. R. *Oasis of Wisdom: The Worlds of the Desert Fathers and Mothers.* Collegeville, MN: Liturgical, 2005.

Keller, Timothy. *Center Church: Doing Balanced, Gospel-Centered Ministry in Your City.* Grand Rapids: Zondervan, 2012.

Kreeft, Peter. *Back to Virtue: Traditional Moral Wisdom for Modern Moral Confusion.* Nashville: Thomas Nelson, 1986.

Lewis, C. S. *Mere Christianity.* New York: Macmillan, 1943.

———. *The Screwtape Letters.* Rev. ed. New York: Scribner, 1996.

MacDonald, James. *Think Differently: Nothing Is Different until You Think Differently.* Nashville: LifeWay, 2017.

Maston, Thomas Buford. *Biblical Ethics: A Survey.* Cleveland: World, 1967.

Matzko-McCarthy, David. *Sex and Love in the Home: A Theology of the Household.* 2nd ed. Eugene, OR: Wipf & Stock, 2011.

Meyer, Joyce. *Battlefield of the Mind: Winning the Battle in Your Mind.* Rev. ed. Fenton, MO: Warner Faith, 2002.

Milavec, Aaron, trans., ed. *The Didache: Text, Translation, Analysis, and Commentary.* Collegeville, MN: Liturgical, 2003.

Moreland, J. P. *Love Your God with All Your Mind: The Role of Reason in the Life of the Soul.* Rev. ed. Colorado Springs, CO: NavPress, 2012.

Norris, Kathleen. *Acedia & Me: A Marriage, Monks, and a Writer's Life.* New York: Penguin, 2008.

Okholm, Dennis. *Monk Habits for Everyday People: Benedictine Spirituality for Protestants.* Grand Rapids: Brazos, 2007.

Olsson, Karl A. *Seven Sins and Seven Virtues.* New York: Harper, 1959.

Patristic Sayings. https://www.patristics.co/sayings/.

Philokalia—The Complete Text. Compiled by Nikodemos of the Holy Mountain and Makarios of Corinth. https://archive.org/stream/Philokalia-TheCompleteText/Philokalia-Complete-Text_djvu.txt.

Piper, John. "What Is the Purpose of Fasting?" *Ask Pastor John,* April 18, 2013. Desiring God. https://www.desiringgod.org/interviews/what-is-the-purpose-of-fasting.

Platt, David. *Radical: Taking Back Your Faith from the American Dream.* New York: Multnomah, 2010.

Postman, Neil. *Amusing Ourselves to Death: Public Discourse in the Age of Show Business.* Rev. ed. New York: Penguin, 2005.

Richardson, Cyril C., trans., ed. *The Teaching of the Twelve Apostles, Commonly Called the Didache.* In *Early Christian Fathers* g. Library of Christian Classics 1. Philadelphia: Westminster, 1953. http://www.ccel.org/ccel/richardson/fathers.viii.i.iii.html.

Routledge, Robin. *Old Testament Theology: A Thematic Approach.* Downers Grove, IL: Intervarsity, 2013.

Schneider, John. *The Good of Affluence: Seeking God in a Culture of Wealth.* Grand Rapids: Eerdmans, 2007.

Seraphim of Sarov. *Little Russian Philokalia.* Vol. 1, *St. Seraphim of Sarov.* Platina, CA: St. Herman of Alaska Brotherhood, 1991.

Shaw, Teresa M. *Burden of the Flesh: Fasting and Sexuality in Early Christianity.* Minneapolis: Fortress, 1998.

Smith, James K. A. *Desiring the Kingdom: Worship, Worldview, and Cultural Formation.* Grand Rapids: Baker, 2009.

Sri, Edward P. "Vainglory: Seeking the Praise of Men." *Lay Witness,* January–February, 2010. Catholic Education Resource Center. https://www.catholiceducation.org/en/education/virtue-education/vainglory-seeking-the-praise-of-men.html.

Thomas, Gary. *Sacred Pathways: Discover Your Soul's Path to God.* Grand Rapids: Zondervan, 2010.

Tickle, Phyllis. "About Fixed Hour Prayer." http://www.phyllistickle.com/fixed-hour-prayer/.

Tilby, Angela. *The Seven Deadly Sins: Their Origin in the Spiritual Teaching of Evagrius the Hermit.* London: SPCK, 2009.

Trollope, Anthony. *Autobiography of Anthony Trollope.* 1883. http://www.literaturepage.com/read/trollope-autobiography.html.

Unger, Merrill Frederick. *What Demons Can Do to Saints*. Chicago: Moody, 1991.

Van den Brink, Gijsbert, and Cornelis van der Kooi. *Christian Dogmatics: An Introduction*. Translated by Reinder Bruinsma with James D. Bratt. Grand Rapids: Eerdmans, 2017.

Waddell, Helen, trans., ed. *The Desert Fathers*. London: Vintage, 1998.

Ward, Benedicta, trans, ed. *The Desert Fathers: Sayings of the Early Christian Monks*. New York: Penguin, 2003.

Wells, David F. *Losing Our Virtue: Why the Church Must Recover Its Moral Vision*. Grand Rapids: Eerdmans, 1999.

Wenzel, Siegfried. *The Sin of Sloth: Acedia in Medieval Thought and Literature*. Chapel Hill, NC: University of North Carolina Press, 2012.

Wilken, Robert Louis. *The First Thousand Years: A Global History of Christianity*. New Haven, CT: Yale University Press, 2012.

Willard, Dallas. *The Divine Conspiracy: Rediscovering Our Hidden Life in God*. San Francisco: HarperCollins, 1998.

Willard, Dallas, and Don Simpson. *Revolution of Character: Discovering Christ's Pattern for Spiritual Transformation*. Colorado Springs, CO: NavPress, 2005.

Winkler, Kyle. *Silence Satan: Shutting Down the Enemy's Attacks, Threats, Lies and Accusations*. Lake Mary, FL: Passio, 2014.

Wortley, John, trans., ed. *The Anonymous Sayings of the Desert Fathers: A Select Edition and Complete English Translation*. Cambridge, UK: Cambridge University Press, 2013.

Scripture Index

EARLY CHRISTIAN WRITINGS

Anthony the Great, 114

Aquinas, 54, 57–58, 80

CPSIA information can be obtained
at www.ICGtesting.com
Printed in the USA
LVHW052349160422
716268LV00003B/46